PRAISE FOR
JOY GIVING

"Most of my professional life has been spent helping Christians plan and manage their financial resources for the glory of God. Cameron, who has traveled the world, brings insight and perspective to the questions they often ask. His book will encourage and challenge each of us. I believe God will use it in a significant way."

— Ron Blue, Founder,
Kingdom Advisors, Georgia, USA

"*Joy Giving* is an excellent resource wherever you are on the journey of giving. The breadth and depth of Cameron's thinking, travel, and research will encourage and inspire you."

— David Smith, Founder,
Genesis Foundation, Sydney, Australia

"*Joy Giving* is the landmark work that only Cameron and Generosity Path could bring forth. This book is a smorgasbord of questions, answers, stories, and fresh, practical biblical insights from God's word and God's people from all over the world. A gift to the global church and to all who want to hear God's heart for giving."

— David Wills, President Emeritus,
National Christian Foundation, Texas, USA

"Cameron Doolittle uses a unique collection of insights from around the world to encourage us to address our questions in a gentle, yet God-inspired way. *Joy Giving* not only helps tease out the answers to our questions, but leads us into a fresh experience of the joy of giving."

— John Preston, National Stewardship and
Resources Officer,
Church of England, London, UK

"This is a veritable storehouse of generosity nuggets, painstakingly mined and collated, a must-read reference for everyone in the global generosity movement. A truly unique achievement is the universal applicability and teachability of the content and the format, transcending human barriers like culture, nation, socio-economic, and other identities."

— Richard Samuel, Director,
CBMC, Madurai, India

"At the Magnolia Foundation, God has given our founders, Chip and Joanna, a great platform for influence. As we've set up the foundation, Cameron has walked with us each step of the way. I've drawn deeply on the principles in *Joy Giving*. We aim to give through trusted relationships, balance giving in our own community with global giving, and focus on organizations purposed to serve holistically. The lessons of *Joy Giving* have shaped our journey and will shape yours."

— Lyle Mason, Executive Director,
Magnolia Foundation, Texas, USA

"Cameron Doolittle has written an outstanding book for followers of Christ who have questions about how God wants them to give. Anchored in hundreds of conversations with givers around the world, this is the practical, biblically based resource that the global Body of Christ has been looking for. I heartily recommend it!"

— Howard Dayton, Founder and CEO,
Compass – Finances God's Way, Florida, USA

"Cameron encapsulates the vast topic of generosity, not just dealing with the 'how' but also with the 'heart' of giving. If Christ is the Lord of my life, then He is the Lord of my finance. I wholeheartedly endorse *Joy Giving* as a practical guide of biblical generosity that will excite anyone who wants to expand God's Kingdom."

— Dr. Francois van Niekerk,
Entrepreneur, Founder of the Mergon Foundation,
and author of *Doing Business with Purpose*,
Pretoria, South Africa

"This is a powerful book on generosity that every pastor, ministry leader, and child of God should read. Cameroon Doolittle shares both biblical and practical wisdom from around the world as he challenges you to do even better walking along your Christian generous path!"

— Andrés G. Panasiuk, General Secretary,
Compass Global Alliance, Florida, USA

"We are responsible for every bit of the money God entrusts to us. Cameron's *Joy Giving* is a timely book by a long-time practitioner. It will help you start the exciting journey to experience deeper joy by giving with eternal impact. A must read for donors and recipients however big or small."

— Suparno Adijanto, Managing Director,
The Bumi Raya Group, Jakarta, Indonesia

"Full of biblical wisdom and practical principles for generous giving, Doolittle does more than merely instruct our minds. He wins our hearts to a powerfully fresh vision of Christian generosity, rooted in the breathtaking generosity of God and whose *telos* is Gospel-centered, joy-filled, global partnership. I will come back to this book often."

— Scott Anderson, President & CEO,
Desiring God, Minnesota, USA

"Read this book with an open heart and an expectant spirit. This journey leads to a destination beyond your wildest imagination. Never making the reader feel guilty, but instead inspiring us to relook at the critical issue of generosity, Cameron encourages us to discover the joy of giving and ultimately acknowledge that generosity has the power to heal what wealth has broken."

— Graham Power, Founder,
Global Day of Prayer and Unashamedly Ethical,
Cape Town, South Africa

"Cameron Doolittle is an experienced, credible herald of the generosity message. Generosity isn't a job or hobby for the Doolittle family; it's a lifestyle and a calling. Having served givers on every populated continent, Cameron's observations on this subject are both practical and inspiring."

— David Denmark, Executive Director,
Maclellan Foundation, Tennessee, USA

"Most money advice encourages you to look inward for answers. This book, and the stories within, will help you to look Godward instead. I've been studying biblical generosity with my whole heart, and I picked up new, fresh insights from this book."

— John Cortines, co-author of
God and Money: How We Found True Riches at Harvard Business School, Florida, USA

JOY
GIVING

Practical Wisdom
from the First Christians
and the Global Church

CAMERON
DOOLITTLE

 Generosity Path

ISBN 978-1-7320927-0-9
eISBN 978-1-7320927-1-6

For more information about this book or the author, visit
HTTP://WWW.GENEROSITYPATH.ORG/

Generosity Path, 820 Broad Street, #300 Chattanooga, TN 37402

Copyediting by Kathy Burge
Cover design by Jenn Reese, Tiger Bright Studios
Interior design by Colleen Sheehan, Ampersand Book Interiors

To Carolyn, Grace, Christiana, Hewson, and Sandhana
Enthusiastic companions and coadventurers
in the joys of giving

TABLE OF CONTENTS

INTRODUCTION
The Questions We're Asking

THE SAME QUIET QUESTIONS echo across the world. In small gatherings of affluent givers. On phone calls. In private dinner conversations. On Skype sessions. The same quiet questions.

From Seoul to London, Stuttgart to Jakarta, and Sydney to Cape Town, when God entrusts His children with wealth, the questions begin.

> *Why did God give us this?*
>
> *What does God want for us and our giving?*
>
> *We know how to make money, but how do we give money in a wise way?*

The questions keep coming.

> *How do we provide for our families without spoiling our children?*

Why isn't there more joy in our giving?

How do we give to our church without the church becoming dependent on us?

Are certain causes more important to God?

How much money is enough?

Is it OK to be rich? And how rich?

Do husbands and wives need to agree on all giving decisions?

Should we give anonymously?

Does giving through a will count as giving?

Is this wealth a test that God expects me to pass?

What if I fail the test?

Perhaps you have asked these questions, even if you don't ask them out loud. Perhaps you don't have a person you trust to answer.

Ask your pastor what to do with your money. He will probably want you to give it all to the church. Even asking the question could change your relationship.

Ask your investment banker. He has an incentive for you to keep it, because his fees come from your assets under his management. Financial advisors are trained to cut your taxes, not grow your eternal impact or your joy in giving.

Perhaps you're not sure what to do, so you give less. It seems better to be passive than to make the wrong move. Perhaps you borrow solutions from investing and take a portfolio approach to giving, measuring the return on your investment.

You keep asking your quiet questions, but the world's answers don't satisfy. They don't bring you joy.

More than giving, more than investing, what we really want is to be fully known and fully loved, not for what we *have* but for who we *are*. God made us with these desires, and yet it's easy to feel isolated. Our wealth isolates us. It makes us unsure who we can trust. It drives us to ask yet another question: *What are the motives of the people around me?*

When people learn about your vacation house, they may become much friendlier. Family members may corner you at the holidays to share a need. This dynamic makes friendship hard, and it makes fellowship hard.

But God can change that. Your wealth can be a tool to bring glory to God, to bring deeper connection to others, to bring unity, and to create adventure and joy.

YOU'RE NOT ALONE

You have found the right place. God loves you, God hears you, and God wants to walk with you and provide answers to your quiet questions. This is the Generosity Path, which has been journeyed by hundreds of global givers who are brothers and sisters in Jesus Christ.

I may not know you personally, but I know the community of Christians around the world whose situations are like yours. As you meet them on the pages that follow, their situations will sound familiar. They will show you that you're not the only one who asks the quiet questions. Even more important, they will assure you that it's possible to be blessed with wealth and also to be fully known and fully loved. They have wrestled with the quiet questions and found answers about the joy and freedom that flow from a life generously lived.

To write this book, I spoke with givers from every populated continent. They come from dozens of countries and speak a variety of languages, which the Generosity Path team carefully translated. The givers make money in various ways: entrepreneurship, inheritance, professions, and investing. They represent many churches, denominations, and strands of the Christian faith. Some are newer believers, and some have walked with Jesus for decades. Together, they are responsible for millions of dollars in annual giving.

These givers share their lives and stories with us at Generosity Path, and our team shares our lives and stories with them. We break bread, travel together, and spend nights in each other's homes. Together, we are part of an unprecedented global generosity movement that is touching thousands of prominent Christians.

Thousands of years ago people sought their own glory at the Tower of Babel, and God scattered them into different languages and geographies. The reverse is now happening. People seeking God's glory are connecting across languages and geographies. The scattered are gathering. The divided are unifying.

I am humbled to bring their stories and insights to you in this book and—hopefully—to welcome you into this joy-filled movement. Bring the quiet questions you've never felt safe to ask; God has drawn together a family of brothers and sisters to answer them. And through this family, He can bring you abundant life and lasting joy.

FROM WHY TO HOW

Across the world, Generosity Path helps Christians answer the *why* of giving. Through an experience we call the Journey of Generosity,[1] people come to understand that Christians are called to give in response to Jesus's amazing gift to us. He gave everything for us, and we want to give generously in response to His generosity.

But Christians also wonder *how* to give.

What does Scripture say about how to give?

How do others who love Jesus give in wise ways?

---

1 The Journey of Generosity was developed by our sister organization, Generous Giving, through the generous support of The Maclellan Foundation.

We don't necessarily want to know how professional philan-thropists organize their giving. We want to know what God wants us to do.

"Scripture, Scripture, Scripture," asserts Oscar from Kenya. "What does Scripture say? We need to talk about this. It's an essential conversation. It is streams in the desert. Pastors here know Scripture, but we need help teaching it to our wealthy givers." Global givers are not looking for best practices from the Western world, but for proven principles from the Word of God.

In other words...

More Romans, less Rockefeller.

More Galatians, less Gates.

More Philippians, less philanthropy.

The great news is that Scripture is brimming with wisdom, instruction, and examples about how to give. Christians who follow it find—no surprise—that the Word of God is true, it works, and it brings joy.

God has things He wants to say to us about our giving. For example, in Luke 3, people come to John the Baptist and basically ask *what should we do? How do we repent and turn to God?* John responds to three different groups with three different commandments, but his guidance is always about money and possessions. Conversion seems connected to currency. Perhaps he knew something about the relationship between our stuff and our heart.

Tax collectors ask, "What should we do?" and John says, "Don't collect any more than you are required to" (Luke 3:12-13).

Soldiers ask, "And what should we do?" John says, "Don't extort money...be content with your pay" (Luke 3:14).

John tells the people, "Anyone who has two shirts should share with the one who has none, and anyone who has food should do the same" (Luke 3:11).

What does God say that we should do?

THE GENEROSITY PATH AHEAD

Jesus wants to talk to us about money. As we study His guidance in Scripture and discern what He wants it to mean for us, those on the Generosity Path find unspeakable joy, freedom, and deeper relationships with Him.

Each chapter of this book addresses questions I've heard from givers like you. I'll look at those questions first, while also encouraging you to ask different questions. We will look to the early church for examples and answers, and we'll see how the Gospel influenced the world's first Christians to give. And then we'll see whether these biblical principles and practices can work in today's world.

Interwoven with the questions and answers, we'll hear personal stories and practical wisdom from global Christian givers. We'll hear how they put Scripture's principles into practice, and what they've learned from their own experiences.

Along the way, I believe you'll find that the Bible's approach is better than the world's and that its teaching is relevant to the questions we ask today. When Christians follow Scripture, their giving differs from the world and leads to deeper joy and greater eternal impact.

Please note that this is a book about financial generosity, but there are absolutely other ways to be generous. Generosity *always* involves more than money. I love "whole life" generosity and believe every Christian should give not just financially but out of their time and their expertise, as well. But the givers I know say that other kinds of generosity don't seem as vexing. They know how to volunteer and how to be hospitable. So this book focuses on financial giving.

Scripture has a lot to say about money, and so does this book. Let's explore the answers you're looking for. Your Creator designed you to experience joy in your giving. He loves to give, and He designed you to love it too.[2]

---

2 All of the stories I tell below are real. But I've changed most of the names to protect our friends' privacy.

1: PURPOSE

What Are Our Reasons for Giving?

"I HAD LEFT AN unethical company to start a new company," says Kim, who now manages a financial advisory firm in Korea. "I'd taken risks for God, and things with the new company were difficult. More difficult than I'd thought."

He became frustrated with God, to the point of tears. "I said, 'God, you put me in this industry. Why did you have me start this company? Why don't you have mercy on me?'

"Then one night, God appeared to me as I was asleep in bed. He appeared to me and asked me two times, 'Who is the owner of your life? Who is the owner of your life?' And then he asked me, 'Who is the owner of your money?'

"I actually wasn't sure. So I woke up my wife and said, 'Who is the owner of our money?' and she said, 'God is.' She was right!"

That knowledge changed everything about Kim's business and the way he advised his clients. It also changed his giving.

"We encourage the people [we advise] to know that the Lord is generous. We can see blessing and contentment in our generosity."

Kim talks about this shift as being like a second conversion experience.

God asks us the same question Kim confronted: *Who is the owner of your life?*

When we realize that He is the owner, we are free to give. We know that God so loved the world that He *gave*. We so love God that *we* give.

In pursuit of purposeful giving, Jose from Costa Rica asked himself the question millions are asking: *Now that I've got some wealth, why did God give me this? And what am I supposed to do with it?*

We know that life is short. "When I was a kid, I never went to funerals," says Lucas in Latin America. "Now, we go to funerals all the time. Our country has become violent. At funerals, you realize that they're not taking anything with them. He owns everything. That's bedrock."

We want to give to God, but it seems complicated. There are so many ways to give. There are so many needs, so many causes, so many asks.

Each of us must determine the purpose of our own financial giving. We must discover what God wants us to do with the wealth He has entrusted to us, and then we must obey.

The path to joy giving is open-handed obedience. "If people really knew what the Scriptures say about how to give," says my Nigerian friend Abaeze, "and if we believed what they say, then we would move radically toward obedience."

VLAD'S STORY: FROM FEAR OF MONEY TO FREEDOM IN GIVING

Vlad is a prominent businessman in central Europe who, over time, grasped the message found in the Scriptures and moved radically toward obedience. "When I accepted Christ, I took the camel and the eye of the needle very literally. I thought I was not supposed to be rich. We started a business, and I actually was kind of afraid that we would be successful. We decided to give away 50 percent of the profits. But as time went by, I did not keep that promise. I drifted from God."

The business grew dramatically. Vlad won awards and earned profits as a wildly successful entrepreneur. "Then I came back to God," Vlad says. "When I did, I wrestled with this question of 'why generosity?' I asked God. I said, 'God, how do you want me to serve you, and what are you calling me to do?'

"I realized that God entrusted me with this money to be a blessing to others."

Vlad decided to make a list of reasons for giving. He emailed the list to me, and I'm including it here in his own words:

- Because God loves us so much, He first gave us Jesus, who gave everything to us, so we want to give as well. Our giving is a reflex response to the grace of God in our lives.

- We affirm that the purpose of wealth entrusted to us is to be a blessing for others. God blessed us so we can be a blessing for others.

- We affirm that we are only stewards of what was entrusted to us by God. God owns everything. We are His money manager.

- Giving brings us joy and a sense of purpose. Giving is in line with our calling and the good works God has prepared for us (Ephesians 2:10).

- Giving is an eternal investment. By giving, we store up our heavenly treasure (Matthew 6:19-21). Not earth, but heaven is our country (Hebrews 11:16).

- Giving brings us closer to God.

- Giving is an act of worship.

- Giving is the only antidote for materialism.

- In Jesus, we have everything (Matthew 6:33), so we can give freely of our possessions.

These are all great reasons to give!

Based on his list, Vlad developed the following purpose statement for his giving: "Invest resources—money, time, personal talents, and experience—in existing or new strategic Christian projects and people with great impact for potential growth. Mainly in Europe, resulting in many changed lives."

Did you see the best reason on Vlad's list? The most fun reason? The reason that makes all the difference? It was hidden in there.

"Giving brings us joy."

As I talk with givers around the world, I can predict their joy by listening for one thing: the language of beauty, rather than the language of duty.

Giving is a response to beauty, not an act of duty.

Christopher in South Africa helps some of the world's wealthiest people with their giving. He says, "When they come to me, most of them haven't addressed *what does God really want?* They still give based on guilt or based on whatever proposals happen to come in."

Christopher's friends in South Africa are giving as an act of duty, not as a response to God's beauty. But Jesus says, "It is more blessed to give than to receive" (Acts 20:35, NIV). More blessed means more happy, more whole, more joyful, more fun.

Jesus appeals to joy, to delight! This is the language of beauty. This is the motive for our giving.

YOUR REASONS FOR GIVING

Before we continue on, take a moment to pray. Ask the Father, "What are my reasons for giving?" List what He shows you below.

THE LANGUAGE OF DUTY

When you think about giving, what kind of language do you use: duty or beauty? It's easy to slide into the language of duty. Let's hear a bit more of it so you can learn to recognize it. Then, when the Enemy whispers *duty* to your heart, you'll be able to intercept it.

- *Duty can sound like a twisted view of our Father.* One man in Africa told me he started giving because "there is an awesome curse of God in not tithing. I was under a curse since I was not tithing." He believed His Father was cursing Him.

- *Duty can sound like hard and fast rules.* Many Christians believe that giving God ten percent will satisfy Him. Some cite Old Testament phrases about "robbing God" by giving less than a tithe. Once they've given ten, they think they can do whatever they want with the other ninety percent.

- *Duty can sound like a penalty.* Janice, who lives in Southeast Asia, shares that in her area "money is often derived from corruption. We are only told in church about the negative sides of money, so we try to pretend we don't have it. We are made to feel guilty for having wealth. Money equals corruption equals greed equals sin. No one tells us what God wants us to do. Some people give away some money so that they don't feel as bad about the money that they get from corruption."

- *Duty can sound like giving money so we get more money.* The language of duty appears in the so-called prosperity gospel, which shifts the duty onto God. It says, "God, I'm giving you something, so you are bound to give me something later." Amit in India says, "Most people who teach on giving are teaching 'give so that God will give you back tenfold.' India's big need related to generosity is to stop listening to that teaching."

SCRIPTURE EMBRACES BEAUTY, NOT DUTY

Duty weighs on us. It feels heavy. So when we hear it, we must consider what Scripture teaches. Jesus rebuked the Pharisees because they "tie up heavy burdens, hard to bear, and lay them on people's shoulders," and through this guilt-tripping, they "devour widows' houses" (Matthew 23:4 and Mark 12:40).

Throughout the New Testament, Peter and Paul encouraged generosity. If they wanted to be legalists about it, they had every opportunity to do so. But they did not set percentages. They did not shame people.

They avoided the language of duty. They chose the language of beauty.

Just one example: in 2 Corinthians 9, Paul is eager to raise money for missionary work and to help needy saints in Jerusalem. But he doesn't appeal to guilt, shame, or duty. Instead, here's what he says:

> *You will be enriched in every way so that you can be generous on every occasion, and through us your generosity will result in thanksgiving to God. This service that you perform is not only supplying the needs of the Lord's people but it is also overflowing in*

many expressions of thanks to God. (2 Corinthians 9:11-12, NIV)

Paul seeks givers who are motivated by "many thanksgivings to God" and people who "glorify God" (2 Corinthians 9:13). God is at the center of Paul's purpose, not a sense of guilt or duty.

Look back at the reasons for giving that you wrote down. Do they sound like duty or beauty?

YOUNG'S STORY: A HEAVENLY JOY

Now that we've heard the language of duty and learned to identify it, let's listen to the opposite. What does the language of beauty sound like? Young, an attorney in Korea, tells this story:

"About five years ago, I wanted to be a senior partner at our firm. I was praying about it a lot. At the same time, a boy in my daughter's school suddenly became an orphan due to a car accident. I didn't know him, but my wife had just told me about him.

"I kept praying to God about becoming a senior partner, but each time I did, He kept reminding me of the orphan. It became so vivid in my mind. I tried to focus on my prayer for myself, but it became more and more vivid. I didn't even know [the boy's] name, but God kept making the story alive in my mind. He gave me a desire to help this person, and I literally could not pray for anything else.

"I thought, 'If I mention this to my wife, she will look at me strangely,' so I used that as a way to tell if this was from God. I said, 'I will consider this as your instruction, Lord, if my wife is supportive.'

"So I said one small thing to my wife. 'By the way, honey, you mentioned about that boy…' and she immediately said, 'You want to help him? I thought you would want to help.'

"I suggested an amount we could give, and it was the amount that she had thought. We thought that it came from God. We gave it anonymously through the school, which gave it to the social worker. Everyone was very grateful and quite moved.

"Then the strangest thing happened. I was driving to work. About halfway there, I thought about the story, about the boy. All of a sudden, I was struck by the joy. I was almost trembling. I couldn't drive. I had to stop my car. I waited and waited. I just couldn't drive. I still remember. It was almost a heavenly joy. The kind of joy we will have when we see Jesus face to face. I realized that God gave me that joy."

THE LANGUAGE OF BEAUTY

Do you want the kind of joy that God gave Young? You can, when you recognize and respond to the language of beauty.

You *get* to give, not you *have* to give.

You *may* give, not you *must* give.

Giving from beauty, not giving from duty.

Like Young, other global Christian givers also speak the language of beauty:

- "Giving is a joyous thing. You get God's joy, and you get to give God's joy to others! It almost feels selfish." (Latin America)

- "God's heart is a generous heart. Enjoy being part of that!" (India)

- "We know the richest man in the whole universe, we belong to Him, and He lets us use His money." (China)

We *get* to give. God gives us all we need, and then He gives us joy.

TWO BENEFITS TO GENEROSITY: FREED *FROM* AND FREED *TO*

Generosity frees us *from* and frees us *to*.

Through giving, we're freed from the love of money. Hebrews 13:5 (NIV) says, "Keep your lives free from the love of money and be content with what you have...."

Those who desire to be rich fall into temptation, and into many senseless and harmful desires that plunge people into

. and destruction. "For the love of money is the root of all kinds of evils" (1 Timothy 6:10).

"Generosity changed us," says a friend in China. "Before, money was like a burden. It's like we were slaves to money. Our temper, our mood, it's like we were slaves. But we don't want to live like slaves. Now there's freedom!"

Wealth might look like a resort, but it can be a prison. Scripture tells us to be careful. Giving sets us free from the love of money, and free from the pain greed causes.

Generosity frees *from* the love of money, but God has another gift for us.

Through giving, we are freed *to* glorify God.

Do you ever wish God would do miracles through you? I'd love to have more miraculous power in my life, like when Jesus healed a paralyzed man and "amazement seized" everyone so they "glorified God and were filled with awe" (Luke 5:17-26). Wouldn't it be great to help bring that kind of reaction to God?

Great news: that's exactly what happens when we give to God. When the Corinthians gave, Paul said that people would glorify God in response such generosity: "You will be enriched in every way to be generous in every way, which…will produce thanksgiving to God" (2 Corinthians 9:11).

Could our generosity really point people to God? Could we really participate in God-glorifying miracles? Scripture repeatedly says *yes, yes, yes!*

Let your light shine before others, so that they may see your good works and give glory to your Father who is in heaven (Matthew 5:16).

As each has received a gift, use it to serve one another, as good stewards … in order that in everything God may be glorified through Jesus Christ (I Peter 4:10–11).

Somehow our giving brings God glory. Others see our giving, and their hearts turn to God. What a beautiful opportunity! We give, and He gets glory. What a mystery. What a miracle.

THE BEST KINDS OF GIVING

If the purpose of our giving is to bring God glory, we need to ask what kinds of giving bring Him the most joy, the most glory.

As we begin to give, *any giving* is better than *no giving*. *Any giving* is a step in the right direction toward breaking the power of money in our lives. *Any giving* could show that we put others' needs ahead of our own.

But God isn't just trying to free us from the love of money. He wants that money to do something. He wants our generosity and hospitality to be given liberally and lavishly, not indiscriminately. The *best* giving we can do points people toward Him.

There are passages in 2 John and 3 John that capture a bit of God's heart for Gospel-centered giving. At the time of John's writing, there was a heresy going around that Jesus hadn't really come to earth as a man. John reminds "the elect lady" to whom he is writing (2 John 1) that Jesus came in the flesh (2 John 7) and then warns her about people who spread heresy. He says, "If anyone comes to you and does not bring this teaching, do not receive him into your house or give him any greeting, for whoever greets him takes part in his wicked works" (2 John 10–11).

If all giving, and all hospitality, were of equal value, John would not warn his reader against welcoming these false teachers.

By contrast, in 3 John, John is writing to Gaius and encourages him to support "brothers" who "have gone out for the sake of the name" since they are "fellow workers for the truth" (3 John 5–8).

Financial gifts can be generous *and yet not glorify God*—they can even undermine His work.

So when you have an opportunity to give, ask God how He wants you to use the money He's given you. When does He want His money to directly support the spread of His word in the world? When does He want you to give more broadly?

Consider Jesus's own generosity with his time. He had infinite power to heal, and yet He allowed people all over the world to remain sick even as He walked the earth. Millions of people passed away during His three years of ministry. Why?

Because Jesus's purpose was not just to reduce human physical suffering but to welcome lost people into His family. The healing was not the point; the Healer was.

We see this clearly in Luke 4, after Jesus healed a lot of people and cast out demons. The crowd asks him to do more, but He surprises them. He declines to do more works of mercy or to heal more people. Instead, He says that He's going to preach "the good news of the kingdom of God to the other towns as well; for I was sent for this purpose" (Luke 4:40-43).

Physical healing was not Jesus' purpose. His purpose was to preach the good news. He did good works in order to point to God. He healed to point to the Healer. He gave to point to the Giver.

Let's return to my friend Vlad, introduced earlier in this chapter. When I asked him about the purpose of giving, he wrote: "The ultimate blessing for people is to come to Christ, in personal relationship with him, to grow in Him, and finally to be with Him forever in heaven."

Vlad's giving points to the Giver.

Any giving can press back the darkness of our fallen world. Meeting physical needs is good, but physical healing is not the heart of God's purpose.

A gift that leads someone to thank you or to thank a non-governmental organization may be a *good* gift. But it becomes a *great* gift when it leads someone to thank God and seek to know Him. Following Jesus's example gives us a purpose for our giving.

THE BIBLE CONNECTS FINANCIAL GIVING TO JOY ON EARTH AND IN ETERNITY

Scripture whispers secrets to us about heaven. It tells us our actions on earth affect our eternity, and it loves to talk about storing up treasure for the next life.

> *Do not lay up for yourselves treasures on earth, where moth and rust destroy and where thieves break in and steal, but lay up for yourselves treasures in heaven, where neither moth nor rust destroys and where thieves do not break in and steal. For where your treasure is, there your heart will be also (Matthew 6:19-21).*

Jesus says our treasure and our heart go together. This operates in two ways:

1. At the eternal level, as we send treasure ahead to heaven, we think more about heaven. Our anticipation grows.

2. At the earth level, we know that treasures and hearts travel together. If we invest in a company like Alibaba or Apple, we become more interested in them. Giving is the same. We care about the places where we send money. Our hearts attach to Vietnam as we give to missions there. We pray more for it.

We know that generosity brings joy now, but Jesus shows us that it also brings eternal riches. Most people are generally more excited about experiencing joy now, but Scripture seems more excited about eternal riches. Maybe the authors know something we don't! Consider:

- Jesus says to store up treasure in heaven. Eternal riches are not destroyed (Matthew 6).

- Paul says the rich should be generous and ready to share. This way they store up treasure for themselves as a firm foundation for the future so that they can take hold of "life that is truly life." (1 Timothy 6:18-19, NIV).

- Jesus says "Your Father has been pleased to give you the kingdom." So since you're getting the kingdom, "sell your possessions and give to the poor. Provide purses for yourselves that will not wear out, a treasure in heaven that will never fail" (Luke 12:32-33, NIV).

- Paul talks to the Philippians and encourages them to give. Why? He doesn't "seek the gift, but I seek the fruit that increases to your credit" (Philippians 4:17).

- Jesus tells us to love our enemies. Fair enough. But He also tells us to lend to them. Really? "Expecting nothing in return, and your reward will be great, and you will be sons of the Most High" (Luke 6:35).

Those who invest only in this life will come to regret it. Jesus tells us about the rich fool who had had so much that he didn't know what to do with it all. He built larger barns to hold his goods. "But God said to him, 'Fool! This night your soul is required of you, and the things you have prepared, whose will they be?'" (Luke 12:20). Tragic.

What's the point of money? Jesus tell us that it's to build up treasure for eternity. In Luke 16:1-13, he tells the parable of the shrewd manager. I didn't fully understand this passage until my Norwegian friend Gisle pointed something out: "Financial capital helps us build relationships with others and with God. That's the whole purpose." Let's see what he means.

A worker is about to get fired. Before he goes, he tries to earn the favor of those others who may hire him. He finds people who owe money to the boss, and he reduces their bills.

Clearly, the lesson is not about being a good employee! Instead, it's about how to exchange something we're losing for something we can never lose.

You, too, may be holding onto something you're losing, but God is giving you the chance to exchange it through giving.

Jesus concludes, "Make friends for yourselves by means of unrighteous wealth, so that when it fails they may receive you into the eternal dwellings" (Luke 16:9).

What does He mean by unrighteous wealth? He's talking about this world's currency. Jesus talks about *when* wealth fails, not *if* it fails.

Not long ago, I sat with a group of believers in Budapest. All of them were from former communist countries. They each told stories about how traumatic it was when the Eastern Bloc regimes fell and their currency became worthless. The same will happen to each of us one day.

The world thinks of money as precious. Jesus, who knows about *true* riches, dismisses all of our money as "unrighteous wealth" that doesn't even compare to the true wealth He has for you in heaven.

Someday we will see true beauty and true glory, and we will laugh at ourselves—or maybe weep—for not investing more in things that last. Once we cross to the other side, our currency will be worthless to us. So our purpose should be to use it soon and use it for the right things. This is the path to joy on earth and riches in heaven.

What are the right things? Things that bring glory to—and gratitude toward—God.

Now that you have thought about your reasons for giving, revise the reasons you wrote earlier. In light of this chapter, why do you want to give?

Our purpose frames the questions we will explore together in the chapters ahead. We will talk about how much to give and to whom.

God allows us tremendous freedom in these areas, because regardless of the *outlet* for our giving, the *outcome* points to the ultimate Giver. And that Giver designed you to experience joy giving, just as He does.

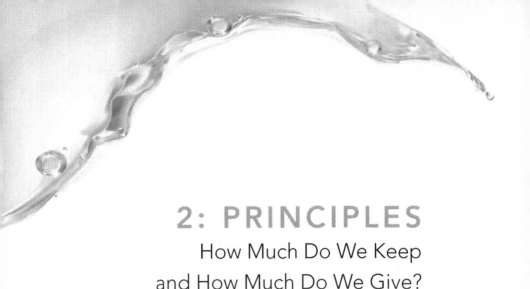

2: PRINCIPLES
How Much Do We Keep and How Much Do We Give?

ZHANG, A CHINESE CEO, owns a company that competes with Alibaba and generates a lot of cash. He's just over five feet tall, with spiky black hair, eyes that look like he's just seen fireworks for the first time, and the smile of someone falling in love. When he came to Christ four years ago, God began changing everything about Zhang's life.

Today, joy flows from him. Zhang hosts Bible studies, prayer meetings, and church services for his employees. He understands the purpose of giving to bring glory to God and to point people to the Giver. His heart is on fire, and Zhang wants God to light a fire in others' hearts too.

As he and I were talking, assistants came in and out of his office, bringing him tea and dropping memos on his desk. In

the midst of that busy space, he surprised me with a simple question.

"What's a good amount for me to give away?" he asked. "I still own seven percent of my company. How much of it should I give away?"

Zhang isn't the first person to ask this question. Givers around the world ask *how much* in various ways.

Every time we have a coin or a bank balance, we have a choice to give, save, or spend. We want guidelines, so we ask: *What's for God and what's for me?*

Sophie in Switzerland says, "The hardest question is 'how much is enough?' Some people are happy living in a flat with no car, just bikes. Others need more. Is it really a sin? Is it bad? What is too much? Could I give more? Of course. But how much is enough?"

Many givers want a formula or number, but the answer is not necessarily easy, nor should it be. Math cannot resolve what is ultimately a matter of the heart. Our giving should be based on an ongoing conversation. That's the joy: talking to your Father every day, about every transaction.

Back to my conversation with Zhang. He owned seven percent of the company and had already allocated two percent of that to God. That's 29 percent of what he made and owned. He wanted to know if that was a good percentage.

"Zhang," I said, "it's great that you love God and want to honor Him. But I can't tell you if 29 percent is good or bad. How did you get to that number? What are you sensing God telling you? If He is asking you for more, 29 percent is bad, but if He is asking you for 29 percent, then it's good."

Zhang reflected for a moment, and then he nodded. He was at peace. Zhang had given God the portion God asked him to give.

LICENSE, LEGALISM, AND LISTENING

Without an easy answer to the *how much* question, our hearts may drift to one of two extremes: license or legalism.

License gives us permission to decide entirely on our own. It says *God gave us this wealth, so we can do whatever we want with it.*

Legalism, on the other hand, demands that we follow strict rules. It says *we must give away some specific amount to be OK with God.*

But there's a land between license and legalism. It's the land of listening.

We know we should give generously. We also know that God must be OK with us keeping some money to use for ourselves. Each of us must choose to share and to keep amounts between nothing and everything. Navigating the land of listening means walking through these choices with simple dependence.

Richard Foster writes about this simplicity in *Celebration of Discipline*: "The inward reality of simplicity involves a life of joyful unconcern for possessions. Neither the greedy nor the miserly know this liberty. It has nothing to do with abundance of possessions or their lack.... I have discovered that often those who have [money] the least love it the most."

Many givers look for numeric or lifestyle guardrails to guide their giving, but they often look in the wrong places. God isn't looking for us to all give the same specific percentage. He doesn't outlaw specific possessions or keep a list of car brands that are OK—and not OK—for His children to own. He doesn't say that it's fine to take four weeks of vacation a year but not six weeks, or two weeks but not four. As we look for guardrails and examples of how much to give, our hearts can drift back to legalism. Well-intentioned guidelines often shout louder than God's still, small voice.

In Nigeria, someone asked my friend Abaeze, "What percentage should I give?" When Abaeze told him to ask God, the man replied, 'I know I can trust you, though. What percentage should I give?"

Abaeze responded, "It's not a question of the amount of money so much as the obedience. When that is understood, it's not how much we give, but how much we keep."

If guidelines help us make decisions without robbing us of joy, that's great. But before we start calculating percentages, making specific purchases off-limits, or looking to tax regulations for benchmarks, let's turn to Scripture and the guidance we find in God's Word.

TWO TAX COLLECTORS, TWO DIFFERENT RESPONSES, BOTH APPROVED BY JESUS

The Gospel of Luke tells the stories of two tax collectors who decide to follow Jesus. They both respond with outrageous generosity, but in different ways—and Jesus approves of both.

In Luke 5, Jesus sees a man named Levi and says to him, "Follow me." Levi leaves everything, including his lucrative job as a tax collector, to follow Jesus. Then he throws a huge party—a "great banquet in his house"—with a "large crowd of tax collectors" (Luke 5:27-29, NIV). Levi's changed heart leads to outrageous, generous hospitality. He responds with money, sharing his wealth in order to give his colleagues a chance to meet Jesus.

But Zacchaeus responds differently. In Luke 19:1-10, we see Zacchaeus, who climbs a tree to get a better view as Jesus passes through town. Jesus spots Zacchaeus and says, "I must stay at your house today" (Luke 19:5). Like Levi, Zacchaeus is rich—not only is he a chief tax collector but also a fraudulent one. Like Levi, Zacchaeus responds to Jesus by sharing. But instead of throwing a party, he gives away half his wealth and pays back four times what he gained from the people he wronged.

Two men. Same invitation from Jesus. Same chance to host Jesus in their homes. Same generous hearts. But different responses—one in hospitality toward his friends, and the other in giving to the poor and making restitution.

Jesus didn't ask for a party, nor did He ask for half of Zacchaeus' assets. He left it to each man's heart.

Perhaps God will lead you to Zacchaeus' example of giving away 50 percent. But if 50 percent is giving out of duty rather than beauty, then it's the wrong amount for you.

DISCERNING HOW MUCH TO GIVE

Jesus provides no clear directive about how much to give. Why not?

A commodity trader from Chicago came to a conference on generosity, which Daryl Heald, the founder of Generosity Path, hosted. When Daryl talked about the joy of giving, it didn't square with the trader's experience. After the event, he called Daryl. Without introducing himself, the trader launched into his questions.

"What does this 'experience the joy' mean?" he asked. "Every year, I'm giving away between $3 million and $5 million, and I'm not experiencing the joy."

Daryl asked why the trader wanted to give. The man's answers were mostly about duty and tradition. "My parents taught me to tithe," he said. "They tithe, and so I tithe." The trader shared that he felt obligated to give well beyond a 10 percent tithe, but then he'd have a bad year in trading and would get stressed because he felt had to give a certain amount.

"Well," Daryl said, "then maybe you're not giving."

The man on the phone was combative. "What is that supposed to mean?"

"Look, the issue is not the amount. If you're sincerely seeking God and desiring joy in giving, this is a fruit of the Spirit, and God will answer that. But this is where you need to ask *Him*, not me. I don't have any answers for you." Daryl paused. "But Scripture does."

"OK," said the trader, "so what do I do?"

"Let me send you some verses," said Daryl. "Read these, meditate on them, pray about them, and specifically pray, 'I want joy, Father.'"

So the trader did that for a few months and then came back and requested more verses, which Daryl sent.

As God started to open the trader's eyes through the verses Daryl sent, he got excited, and his wife started to ask what this radical change of heart was about.

"I've been thinking about giving all wrong," the trader said. Over time, he and his wife reached some radical conclusions. They sold their home, worth $8 million, so that they could give more to ministries they loved. Because they wanted to keep their relationships with their neighbors, they moved into a smaller home in the same neighborhood. They knew that their acquaintances gossiped about whether they'd fallen on hard times, but the trader and his wife didn't care.

The trader had always donated money to ministries, but he'd had no relationship with them. Now, he and his family started traveling with these organizations they supported, building relationships with the poor and with those serving the poor.

When Daryl shared this story with me, he said, "I never would have had the faith to tell the trader to give away as much as he did. I couldn't prescribe this solution. But God says, 'Let Me give them the answer.' God spoke to his heart, and the trader found joy."

Paul says, "Each one must give as he has decided in his heart, not reluctantly or under compulsion, for God loves a cheerful giver" (2 Corinthians 9:7). But that begs the question *How do I decide in my heart what to give?*

As we've seen, in the land of listening, God isn't after some fixed percentage of your money, and He isn't trying to hold you to some specific lifestyle. But He does provide you with guidelines. I call them the four filters.

FILTER 1: ENJOYMENT

Our Father loves to give us good gifts. Let that thought sink in for a moment.

We know that God owns everything—He enabled us to earn, build, and accomplish all we have. We also know that

He asks us to be generous, to share. But where is the balance between what to keep and what to give?

Years ago, as I grew in my career and earned more, I had a gnawing sense that I should give it all away. I worried about Scripture passages like the one where Jesus tells the rich young ruler to "go, sell all that you have and give to the poor" (Mark 10:21). I worried about Jesus pointing out to his disciples that the poor widow gave "everything she had, all she had to live on" (Mark 12:44).

These passages led me into dialogue with God: *Is that Your standard? To give it all away?*

I'd heard stories of people who gave away everything in their savings accounts and sold their homes. I wondered if saving for my retirement would someday mean coming up short in my accounts with God.

I didn't know if it was OK to be rich.

But then I read 1 Timothy 6:17, where Paul writes that those who are rich are not to "set their hopes on the uncertainty of riches, but on God, who richly provides us with everything to enjoy."

To enjoy. It's right there in Scripture. When we are careful to set our hope on God, we can enjoy our Father's good gifts.

Many of the people I meet are surprised when they learn that their wealth is a gift to enjoy. But we know that our Heavenly Father loves us. When we love, we lavish gifts upon our beloved. We hope that our beloved enjoys those gifts and uses them well. That's how our Heavenly Father loves us. He loves to provide us with not only enough, but plenty!

A friend recently told me about William, a man who loved fast cars and traveling by private plane. He had mentioned to my friend that he specifically wanted a Porsche racing car and to lease a private jet, but he felt guilty about them—he didn't believe his seemingly extravagant expenses could be God-given desires.

My friend explained that there's not some Bible passage that says Toyota is OK, but Mercedes is bad. If a car and an airplane were the desires of William's heart and he was in the right heart, he should pray. Maybe God would give them to him.

Later, William reported, "I never got peace about the private jet, but I did feel God gave me freedom to buy and race a Porsche."

William held his Porsche with an open hand. "God gave me the freedom to buy it," he says, "but then God said, 'I know you enjoyed it, but now it's time to give it away.' There was a need that came up, and God asked me specifically to meet the need by selling that car. So I did."

God gave William extravagant freedom. He possessed a thing, but the thing didn't possess him.

The Bible doesn't set a standard that we must give away all we have received. Jesus, Paul, and Joseph of Arimathea all show us a balance of what it means to keep and also to give.

Jesus and the disciples were not rich, but they kept a money bag (John 12:6).

Paul also kept enough money on hand that in Acts 24, a Roman official held out for a bribe in exchange for releasing Paul from prison (24:26). Acts closes with Paul living in Rome "at his own expense" and able to welcome "all who came to him" (28:30).

Another example is "a rich man from Arimathea, named Joseph, who had himself become a disciple of Jesus" (Matthew 27:57, NIV). After the crucifixion of Jesus, this man wrapped the dead body of Jesus in cloth and placed it in his own tomb. He risked the wrath of Rome to ask for his friend's body, so we know this was not a nominal Christian. Yet Scripture tells us he was rich.

As we learn to enjoy our Father's good gifts and to let go of idols and guilt, we are ready to consider the next principle that prompts our conversation with God.

FILTER 2: CONTENTMENT

As an older pastor, Paul mentored a younger pastor, Timothy, with whom he shared these beautiful words of insight.

> *But godliness with contentment is great gain, for we brought nothing into the world, and we cannot take anything out of the world. But if we have food and clothing, with these we will be content. (I Timothy 6:6–8)*

Contentment alone is not great gain. But *godliness* with contentment is great gain. Paul goes on to explain what the opposite of contentment looks like:

> *But those who desire to be rich fall into temptation, into a snare, into many senseless and harmful desires that plunge people into ruin and destruction. For the love of money is a root of all kinds of evils. It is through this craving that some have wandered away from the faith and pierced themselves with many pangs. But as for you, O man of God, flee these things. (1 Timothy 6:9–11)*

If we don't find contentment, we end up on the path to "ruin and destruction" and "many pangs."

James, another New Testament writer, paints a disturbingly graphic picture of what those "pangs" might look like. He warns the rich to "weep and howl" because their "riches have rotted," their "garments are moth-eaten," and their "gold and silver have corroded." Those who live "on the earth in luxury and in self-indulgence" have a lot to worry about (James 5:1–5).

Jesus says, "Woe to you who are rich, for you have received your consolation" (Luke 6:24).

These passages are unsettling, and they should be. Those words should drive us to prayer as we ask God to make us content with what we have.

Paul says, "I have learned in whatever situation I am to be content....In any and every circumstance, I have learned the secret of facing plenty and hunger, abundance and need" (Philippians 4:11–12). As for what the secret is, he tells us: "I can do all things through him who strengthens me" (Philippians 4:13). All things! That includes being content.

Nicolas, a giver in France, follows a simple lifestyle. He says, "We commit to look at our budget and think about how we can live on less and give more. But it's so important that we don't make up rules. We need principles, without detailed rules. When Paul talked to Timothy about rich people, he didn't say not to be rich, but he talked about adding other kinds of richness. Adding richness in good work to your richness in money."

The biblical writer of Hebrews tells us, "Keep your life free from love of money, and be content with what you have." We don't just will ourselves to contentment. The sentence finishes, "for he has said, 'I will never leave you nor forsake you'" (Hebrews 13:5).

Contentment in God is our path away from love of money. Contentment outside of God is impossible. Our hearts are not at ease until we find ease in Him.

Gisle in Norway says, "Wealthy people make life so complicated for themselves. What we need to do is step back and talk about how to be content."

As we learn to be content with what we need, we can freely share our resources to help meet the needs of other people. We then come to the next principle.

FILTER 3: FAIRNESS

"Fairness" doesn't mean that everyone ends up with the same amount. Consider the landowner who hired day laborers at various times in Matthew 20 but paid them all the same; each had their needs met, but they were not rewarded in the same ways.

When he writes his second letter to the Corinthians, Paul is raising money. He feels burdened by the needs of the poor saints in Jerusalem, and in chapter 8 he asks his friends to help. But first, he describes how the church in Macedonia, a poorer church, despite a "severe test of affliction," had been blessed through their giving (2 Corinthians 8:1-2).

The Macedonian church is poor, but Paul's Corinthian friends are rich.

Think what tactics we might use if we were in Paul's position, seeking money to help the church in Jerusalem. Would we try to raise as much as possible by telling stories about how the Jerusalem Christians suffer from poverty and hunger? We could use our spiritual authority to guilt the Corinthians into giving. We could ask them to sign a commitment to give a specific amount, or we could suggest a specific monetary goal or target. Perhaps we would be tough on the Corinthians for being so rich.

Paul does none of these things. Instead, he tells a story about the sacrificial generosity of the Macedonians, and then he asks the Corinthians to do what's fair.

Paul tells the Corinthians that the Macedonians, despite their "extreme poverty," have "overflowed in a wealth of generosity" (2 Corinthians 8:2). The Macedonians beg for the chance to help and give beyond their means. Sometimes Paul turns away their money or tells them they've given enough.

Begging means that the Macedonians came back after an earlier attempt was refused. In this situation, it appears that the Macedonians gave generously, experienced joy in giving, and then tried to give more. When Paul attempted to dissuade them, they *begged* for the chance to take part again. They begged to experience the joy of giving.

After telling this story, Paul encourages the rich Corinthians to do what's fair. He says:

> *[Giving] is acceptable according to what a person has, not according to what he does not have. For I do not mean that others should be eased and you burdened, but that as a matter of fairness your abundance at the present time should supply their need, so that their abundance may supply your need, that there may be fairness. (8:12–14)*

As we decide what to give, we might begin by reflecting on stories of sacrificial givers like the Macedonians, but we should also consider what's fair.

Ask God to show you in a situation, "What's fair here? How could our abundance supply others' needs?"

FILTER 4: FAITH

We cannot put these principles into practice without facing the questions:

> Are we depending on our bank accounts? Are we setting our hopes on the uncertainty of riches? Or are we trusting God with what we keep and with what we give?

Scripture tells us to "walk by faith, not by sight" (2 Corinthians 5:7). That means we should give enough that we need to rely on God and give Him opportunity to show His faithfulness.

When I was just out of college, I didn't have much money. I knew what it was like to walk by faith. What I did not know, though, was that stores sold bed frames and mattresses separately. I used all my money to buy a bed frame and then realized that I had no mattress.

And so I prayed, slept on the floor, and waited on God. Within the week, I visited a friend and saw a mattress—just the right size—leaning against a wall. He didn't need it anymore and gave it to me with enthusiasm.

I also needed a suit for my job but didn't have one. So I prayed again, and a friend who visited from the United Kingdom happened to leave a suit behind. When I called to tell him he'd forgotten his suit, he said he didn't need it and I was welcome to it. It fit.

These little lessons built my faith day by day. My Father took care of me when I had nothing.

My friend David, now a successful business owner, remembers the days when he was poor. God miraculously provided for his needs time after time. His faith grew, and his intimacy with God grew. His eyes filled with tears when he told me, "You know, I really miss those days."

A financial planner I know sometimes feels uneasy about her job, because she helps her clients become rich enough that they never need to rely on God. I see her point. Wealth can rob us of the gift of walking by faith. But it doesn't have to.

Paul commends the Macedonian Christians for giving beyond their means and walking by faith. But faith doesn't mean we need to be on the brink of poverty.

I have a friend who set a lifetime giving goal. He told his wealth management firm how much he hoped to give away over the course of his life. They ran the numbers and said, "Sir, we can't figure out a way to get you to that lifetime giving goal." He didn't have enough money to reach the giving goal that God put on his heart.

"Great," said my friend. "Then I think God gave me the right number." He's walking and giving by faith.

We can all walk by faith. The journey will look different for each of us, yet we all have the same Father who loves to give us good gifts.

That's what Jack learned. Jack worked at a hedge fund in London. One day, he came to work and found a note on his desk. When he looked around, he realized that there was a note on everyone's desk.

The notes were from the CEO. "It's been a good ride," the note read. "Thanks for your work. I realized that yesterday was my last day. I shut down the firm and feel like I need to do something different. As a thank you, I'm giving everyone a bonus. It's already been transferred into your bank account."

This was the era before internet banking, so everyone in the company rushed down to the nearest ATM to check their balances.

The ATM spit out Jack's receipt. When he looked down at it, he couldn't believe what he saw. He walked inside the bank and handed the ATM receipt to the teller. "I just checked my balance, and this just can't be right."

The teller started typing. "Sir, that is the correct amount," she said as she slid the receipt back to him.

His balance was more than £50 million, or $70 million at the time.

Jack recounted that he didn't feel elated or relieved. He felt fearful. "What does it look like for me to be sacrificial?" he asked. "I'm not sure I can be a sacrificial giver anymore.'"

In the years since, Jack has been a faithful steward of the fortune that God sent his way. He tries to walk by faith, even in the midst of wild prosperity.

As we walk with God, He will guide how much we should keep and how much to give. He wants us to be content. He is delighted when we share what's fair, and He loves when we rely on Him day by day.

As we pursue joy in our giving, we get to learn from our brothers and sisters around the world who are walking in this joy. In the next chapter, we will see how our friends around the world have built practices and disciplines to help themselves live out these principles as they walk in the joy of giving.

3: PLENTY
What's Extra?

BY THE END OF THE twentieth century, Jean Andre owned one of the largest food companies in Europe. But long before that, when his grain trading business was still small, he visited Germany. Since World War II had just ended, he witnessed poverty and need on a scale he'd never seen. He made a radical decision to bring 120 refugee children to his home in Switzerland, and to ensure that they were fed, clothed, and taught about God's love.

After the first group of children was placed in loving homes, God stirred Jean Andre's heart for deeper generosity. He felt called to do something radical and made a commitment: "All the money I earn personally, I'll divide into two and give half to the Lord."

But Jean Andre knew how quickly his good intentions could fade.

How many promises to yourself have you failed to keep? Every commitment needs *community*. That's why we make our marriage vows publicly. That's why a contract involves signatures from at least two parties. So Jean Andre transparently shared his financial reports with his brother to keep himself on track.

For Jean Andre, half his money was enough for him to live. Anything above that was extra. As his grain shipping business grew, so did his vision, and he found ways to use the "extra" to change thousands of lives. Jean Andre's generosity helped children after World War II in the war-ravaged areas of France, Greece, Austria, the United Kingdom, and Spain. His ministry, Grain of Wheat, founded a children's ministry center near Buenos Aires, Argentina, which still welcomes thousands of children a year. During the 1980s conflicts in Lebanon, Grain of Wheat brought hundreds of children to Switzerland. When the Iron Curtain fell, they did the same for hundreds of Russian children.

Because of Jean Andre's commitment and the accountability to his community to give what was extra, Grain of Wheat has touched the nations with the love of Jesus.

As you discern what's extra, ask Him to lead you to a commitment, and to a community to help you keep that commitment.

SET A GOAL

How do we discern the difference between "enough" and "extra"?

It is easy to think that "extra" is something we'll have later. When I got my first job out of business school, it felt like I was making an impossibly large amount of money. But within months, that impossibly large amount of money felt like "just right," and then quickly it felt like "not enough."

Chen, a giver in China, speaks for many givers. "I used to think that if you have surplus, then that's the time to give to others. But then it seemed like I never had a surplus, even as my business grew. I realized that the time to give is now, with what you have now."

Givers around the world emphasized the importance of being proactive and setting goals. As I talked to them, I discovered that most of their goals could be divided into three types.

A word before we go on: handle the following material with care. While it is *consistent* with Scripture, it is not *mandated* by Scripture. This is advice from our older brothers and sisters in the faith, not God-breathed revelation.

As you prayerfully consider these ways to look at giving, be careful not to impose them on others. These tools are *disciplines* (practices that sharpen ourselves), not *legalisms* (practices that cut others). When we impose our disciplines on others, we quickly lose the joy that God wants us to find in giving.

TOOL 1: LIFESTYLE CAPS

My childhood hero, Steve Largent, was my favorite American football player, then became a US congressman. I worked for him as a speechwriter, and we became friends. Years later, I asked Steve for advice about handling my growing wealth.

He looked at me and said simply, "It's a great question. Here's what you do. Live like it's not there."

It was simple and profound advice.

But how do we "live like it's not there?" Fulton Sheen, late Archbishop of Rochester, once wrote, "Never measure your generosity by what you give, but rather by what you have left."

As givers become generous, they often set—after much prayer—a "lifestyle cap," which is the amount that they believe God gives them to spend on themselves annually. They get to give the rest away as God leads.

Christopher from South Africa explains, "It's not 'what do I give?' Instead, it should be 'What do I keep?'"

Givers don't always give away the rest all at once, but the lifestyle cap protects them from the temptation to spend it. They may set up a separate bank account to collect God's money until He leads them to the right opportunity. An Indian friend told me: "The absence of a conversation about limits leads to an open-ended lifestyle. Do you need a four-bedroom house? OK. Why not freeze it for yourself at four?"

A lifestyle cap is a prayer-driven, self-imposed limit to what we spend on ourselves. It's a great way of "living like it's not there."

John Cortines and Greg Baumer, authors of *God and Money*, did hundreds of interviews with Christian graduates of Harvard University. In the end, they concluded that people, at some point, no matter their income, should limit how much they spend on themselves each month or each year. "Should there be a ceiling on consumption?" they ask. "There is an income above which a Christian's marginal propensity to consume should fall to zero."

Stefan in Germany says that "before, I had never defined 'how much is enough' for me. That was so powerful. Not just 'I give a lot away,' but I give because I have a cap and am following Christ."

Finn in the Netherlands is living this out. "We had two cars, but we asked God and now we have just one car. It was such a joy giving the car away and seeing the blessing this other person has with it. We're trying to shrink the circle to be able to give more away."

Givers generally set up their spending limits in one of two ways.

Fixed Living Amount. Most say, "Of all the money that comes in, our family is going to live on this amount of dollars/

RMB/euros/pounds/etc. and give the rest away. No matter how much comes in, we will live on this set amount."

I have heard fixed living amounts ranging from the median income of a country up to five times that amount (for a family whose children have expensive medical needs). What's important is to ask God "how much is for us" and wait until you have a clear answer from Him.

Fixed Giving Percentage. Others set a percentage: "We will only keep this percentage of what we make."

Saif in Dubai says, "We give a minimum of 20 percent. Above that is gravy. I'm very excited about it."

Roy in the United States says, "We give away 70 percent of our income. We split that three ways: 10 percent to the church; 15 percent to small gifts, like mercy gifts to individuals; and 45 percent to bigger strategic gifts."

Amit in India explains, "I came across teaching that the Old Testament tithe was more than 10 percent. A Jew gave 23.34 percent plus other offerings. That was very touching to me. Under the law, the Jewish people gave 23 percent. How can I give less than that living under grace? That's when I started increasing my giving. Then, of course, the joy of giving makes you increase your giving and not look at the figure, and you end up paying much more than 23 percent. Every year, I endeavor to increase, not just as a percentage, but as a total amount. By God's grace, we have just reached about one third of our income now. Our endeavor is to keep seeing that we can increase."

One ministry I know has a "50-50 Club" in which participants pledge to give away half of what they receive.

Behavioral psychologists tell us that, on the whole, people underestimate what they spend and overestimate what they give. Setting a cap helps us make sure that our treasure actually reflects what our heart wants to do.

TOOL 2: FINANCIAL FINISH LINE

Several givers I talked with set financial finish lines. Where lifestyle caps are about a person's annual rate of spending and income, financial finish lines look at a person's cumulative wealth.

Many givers save until they reach this "financial finish line" and then live on the interest from that. Some, including Vlad in central Europe, reduce their assets year by year. "Our plan is to give away everything," Vlad says. "We are waiting for more specific answers from God, but that is our plan."

To set a financial finish line, givers need to ask: *How large a corpus do I need to live at my lifestyle cap for the rest of my life?*

When "keeping" is our default, we accumulate more and more without actually thinking about what we are saving for. Is it for our children's inheritance? Is it for a big gift from our estate? Daryl Heald explains, "This is foundational.... The scope of what you *can* give dictates everything else. People haven't answered the 'principal' question because they lack planning. If you haven't decided your estate plan and what you're doing with your business, then you can't answer the giving question comprehensively. People can give a lot more once they've taken the time to plan."

Minsoo in Korea says, "God made me rich, but I didn't want to accumulate wealth. My wife and I decided that we have a certain level of wealth, and that is all we need. More than that, we give to God."

Financial planners tell me that their clients are often overjoyed when they look at their entire financial picture and realize how much they can give. One financial planner told me about a client who found out that he could give *three times* more than he had been giving.

Look at your whole financial picture. You may find that you are able to give even more than you thought!

Lifestyle caps and financial finish lines can work together. Let's say you earn $10 per year. You pray and feel led to live on $5, to give $2, and to save $3 each year.

The $5 is your lifestyle cap. You accumulate the $3 per year, letting it grow and increase. Over the years, those $3 annual investments add up and earn interest. Eventually, they generate enough income to cover your $5 lifestyle cap. The amount that generates enough to cover your lifestyle cap is your financial finish line. At that point, you continue living on your $5, giving the initial $2 that you were giving before, and you also get to give away the $3 that you had been saving. You also get to give away any interest that accrues on your investments. Of course, if your investments drop in a given year, you could begin saving again until you reach the financial finish line that God has given you.

While I hope the example above illustrates the principle of how lifestyle caps and financial finish lines work together, don't get stuck in the specifics or see this as prescriptive. The mechanics are not the point; the point is that we've asked God, "How much is enough?" and seize the opportunity to give away the excess.

TOOL 3: ANNUAL AND LIFETIME GIVING GOALS

Many givers take joy in setting an annual or lifetime giving goal.

A friend in Australia set a goal to give away $25,000 in one year, and God provided. Then he aimed for $50,000 and then $100,000. Now he's praying to double that amount again.

Alan Barnhart's company in Memphis, Tennessee, set a goal to give away $1 million a month, and they've been able to do that for more than a decade.

Pastor and author Francis Chan sensed one year that the Lord wanted him to set an annual giving goal of $50,000, even though that was as much as his entire salary as a pastor. He made the commitment in faith, and God provided the resources. In the following years, the Lord challenged Francis to stretch that number to $100,000 and then to $1 million. It seemed impossible—where would a pastor get $1 million? Then, miraculously, his book *Crazy Love* became a bestseller.

In the 1950s, Stanley Tam set a lifetime giving goal of $100 million. That would be almost $900 million in today's currency. By God's grace, he not only hit that number, but he has been able to give much more.

WHAT IS THE RIGHT TOOL FOR YOU?

Giving goals keep us praying and give God the chance to show us how miraculously He provides. When it comes to which tool is right for you, let God lead you. Lay your goals and ideas before the Lord and see if He nudges you in one direction or another. In my family, my wife (Carolyn) and I have found joy in a lifestyle cap and a financial finish line. Some years, the Lord has put an annual giving goal on our hearts, but we've never felt led to a lifetime giving goal.

As you make plans to give your extra, remember you do not need to set your most aggressive goal now. You can adjust your lifestyle cap, finish line, or goal later. Most givers do, in fact.

"I think people need to put their foot in the water and start with a little toe," says Finn from the Netherlands. "Trust and face your fear. We all want to be changed, but the road of change is not easy."

Let's say that today you spend $200,000 annually on your lifestyle. Setting a lifestyle cap of $150,000 may feel difficult. You may be tempted to focus on what you have to give up. You may see a home that you'll have to sell or some part of your lifestyle that you'll miss. I know people whose early forays into generous giving led them to leave expensive health clubs, downsize to small homes, or buy simpler cars. That can hurt.

At first, you may feel like you're trading something for nothing. You may think often about what you're losing. That's natural. The losses feel tangible, and the gains feel ephemeral.

When you have established your tools and pattern for giving, it becomes easier to part with things.

Paul understands. He talks to the Corinthians twice about their giving. In 1 Corinthians 16, Paul is addressing newer believers, so he makes it pretty easy: "On the first day of the week, each of you is to put something aside and store it up" (1 Corinthians 16:2).

Put something aside. *When?* On the first day of the week. *Who?* Each of us. *How much?* Something.

As the years pass, the Corinthians grow in their relationships with God. By the time he writes his second letter, Paul—always a wonderful pastor—can challenge them to greater generosity. He tells the story of the Macedonians to inspire and encourage the Corinthians to "excel" in giving, citing Jesus's example, and calls them to deliver on their generous intent (See 2 Corinthians 8:1-14). They have grown as disciples, so Paul spurs them on—with great love—toward greater generosity.

We don't need to set a radical Stanley Tam $100 million goal today, but we can each prayerfully start somewhere. Then, as we travel down our own generosity paths, we will experience this surprise: we're not trading something for nothing. It's the opposite.

As we give, the images of what we're giving up fade. The images of what we're giving *to* become blindingly bright: baptisms in rivers, people reading the Bible in their own language for the first time, children's lives saved in medical clinics, feeding the hungry, and more.

As we see God use our giving to heal parts of the world and beat back the darkness, we want to do it again. The things that used to feel like sacrifices now barely feel like a sacrifice at all.

A friend in Latin America says, "You get God's joy, and you get to give God's joy to others! It almost feels selfish."

Is it OK to have this much fun?

We're experiencing the joy of the Lord.

As we use the tools, we find that, after a while, they become unnecessary. We have so much fun giving that we want to do it more and more!

Lucas in Latin America explains, "As I see giving start to make things happen, I want to give more. I see God work and ask, 'So what am I going to do now?' I started giving not just from my income, but from my bank account and from my investments. We get to support people and the church in a different way. I say, 'What more do I need?' and 'Do I really need all this?' No, I really don't. You give first, and then your heart follows."

HOW TO MAKE THE GOALS STICK: TRANSPARENCY

It's one thing to set a lifestyle cap or a financial finish line or a giving goal. It's another thing to stick to it.

Our friends around the world have shown us the value of bringing our giving to others for accountability. We all need relationships like Jean Andre had with his brother. When the conversation and community are absent, our hearts are quick to spend on ourselves. When we involve just one other person, we are more likely to keep our commitments.

With so much of our culture telling us to buy new things and new experiences, we need to surround ourselves with voices who remind us of things that are true and right and eternal. Liam in Australia says, "There are all these toys you can spend money on, so we, as a group, say, 'We can spend dollars instead on being generous and giving it away.'"

"How much we pay ourselves [as business owners] is one of the biggest challenges," says Rahul in India. "There are some guys that submit their accounts to their peers, who determine what level of salary they should pay themselves. That's amazing. I submit myself to a peer group that counsels me and says, 'Your lifestyle is here.'"

Of course, if you involve others, you need to be sure that you're prepared to follow their guidance. Accountability isn't real until it makes us do something we prefer not to do. Until accountability costs us something, it's just a way of validating our own preferences. Accountability without submission is no accountability at all.

My friend Joe was in an accountability group based on the rule "you can ask me any question you want." The group had been meeting for many years when one guy walked in and threw sheets of paper on the table. Everyone knew immediately what the spreadsheets were about.

"This is the one card we've never played," he said. "If we're willing to hold each other accountable on these other things, why not money too?" He might be fine on the rest of life, he explained, but he felt like he was failing at stewarding God's money. "If I trust you guys to speak into my life, why can't I trust you to speak to me about how much I should live on?"

He went on to explain his financial life in detail. "I give myself a C grade right now," he said, "and I want to do better."

Isolation is dangerous. If you don't have a trustworthy friend, consider finding a Christian financial advisor. We are always better walking together in the light.

WARNING: GIVING MORE CAN HURT YOUR EGO

"That's it? You must have more than that." A financial advisor was sitting with my friend Phillip, looking at his financial statements.

"No, that's all I have," Phillip said.

Phillip had been successful in business but chose a path of generosity. He tithes, gives sacrificially, and pours out his life and income for Gospel advancement. Phillip chooses not to be rich. Despite his education, capabilities, and family wealth, he chooses radical. In that moment, though, across the table from his advisor, Phillip felt a flash of shame.

Have you felt it? Your kids seem to wear the same clothes more often than their friends. Your colleagues take nicer vacations. Embarrassment creeps in. Let's call it "the shame of less." You've chosen to be generous. By definition, when you give you end up with less than you would have had; but since our hearts still want to use money and possessions as a scorecard, as a measure of value. That's the "shame of less."

Phillip has now learned that God wants the shame of less to become what we might call "the game of less," the joyful experience of remembering that, *because* we've chosen less, someone else has much more.

Alan has prospered financially but lives on a fraction of his income so he can give to God's global cause in missions. His son, eleven-year-old Nathan, once told him, "Dad, I think we should get a Hummer."

Alan paused. "Nathan, that's a great idea. What if we got two Hummers? I could do that for you. I could buy you enough Hummers to fill up our whole driveway. But if we don't buy those Hummers, we can take that money and give it to people who don't know where they're going to get their next meal or don't have any access to the Gospel."

If God gives Alan freedom to have a Hummer, that's great. If Alan's job requires a Hummer, no problem. But Alan knows that there are tools and there are toys.

Tools are things that we need to have in order to serve others. Someone who owns a theater also owns a very expensive sound system. It's a tool. For someone else, the same sound system is a toy. Alan chooses to own less, and with it, he receives greater joy. The shame of less has become the game of less.

I call it a game because, over time, it becomes fun to remind ourselves *why* we have less—that having less is what opens the door to having more joy and more fellowship.

Hebrews says Abraham lived by faith because he was "looking forward to the city...whose architect and builder is God" (Hebrews 11:10, NIV). Similarly, rather than a luxurious life in Egyptian palaces, Moses chose the heavenly country (Hebrews 11:16).

When we're following God's direction, we can look at the things of this life and compare them to the things of the next, and then find that it's no contest.

In our home, my family and I live comfortably. God has given us many good gifts to enjoy. But God showed us that our lifestyle and our net worth is enough.

Once we made that decision, Carolyn and I still had surges of covetousness. I was visiting a friend in Washington, DC, who mentioned that he had bought a second home in Minnesota.

My flesh said, "Hey, I should buy a second home in Minnesota." Now, at the time, I had never even been to Minnesota, but my heart was moving in.

We think, "I want one like that" and "my clothes could be newer" and "we could get a nicer car" and "we really should go to Italy sometime."

But the more we give, the less control the love of money has over us. As we learn to love the game of less, moments of greed can become moments of gratitude. I can see a luxury car and think, "Thank You, God, for the chance to give to that school in the Himalayan foothills that's spreading the Gospel."

Moments of wanting can become moments of worship. I can see an ad for a cruise and think, "God, how amazing that you would use people like us to buy land for that orphanage in the Dominican Republic."

Moments of empty desire can become moments of delight. Grasping becomes granting, and coveting becomes contributing. And the joy that results is profound and rich. My wardrobe is smaller, but I rejoice that, instead, there's a new church ministering on the outskirts of Lima.

I love the Tour de France. Two hundred bike riders compete each year, but few have a real chance to win the champion's yellow jersey. Most don't even compete for it. Instead, many strive to be best sprinter, best at climbing mountains, best young rider, etc.

The Tour de France is long, with twenty-one days of racing. Riders who have no shot at the yellow jersey sometimes try to win a single day. They sprint ahead, putting everything into what's right in front of them, but the true contenders for the yellow jersey don't worry. They don't care if a rider wins Day 12.

To marginal fans, the Day 12 winner looks like the champion. He's not. The true contenders compete for a different prize.

Generous givers ask themselves what prize they are competing for. When they see someone who seems to "get ahead" in life, they don't try to catch up. Instead, they remind themselves that they are in a different race, competing for a different prize—a heavenly one.

As God provides abundantly, He gives us the joy of giving. As we ask Him, "What's for me, and what's for me to share with others?" we experience joy in the conversation with Him, finding contentment not in His gifts, but in the Giver.

Once we've decided how much to give and developed processes for ensuring that we hold ourselves accountable, we get to think about where to give these gifts. It's about to get fun!

4: PASSIONS
God's Passions and Mine

JAMES WAS A FARMER in Australia. "It's funny," he says. "Farming families are asset rich but often cash poor. I'm the sixth generation on the farm, and the farm's always been worth a lot. But we didn't have a lot of income."

James felt the call toward giving, though. "Even as a teenager, I remember going up to some guy after a mission talk at church and saying, 'What's more important—to go or to be resourced to go?' Even though we didn't have a lot to give, I thought that [the spiritual gift of giving] might have been a spiritual gift that we've been given." James has ended up being a resource to many ministries; sometimes he "goes" but usually he gives.

Over the last few years, God has given James a profound passion for a specific mission in India. It began when his childhood friend Robert began a series of health clinics in

the Himalayas. The more Robert talked about his vision for sharing Jesus through the clinics, the more excited James got.

"As we started to give more generously, we became more passionate and more strategic as givers.... Robert has always been a good investment. He's a good friend and trustworthy, with a cost-effective model, very strategic, working in a key place." James began helping Robert raise funds from others. Eventually James decided to go see the projects for himself.

"I took our sixteen-year-old son along to see it," James says. "We saw the programs and the health centers. I was really keen to see Robert's work. It confirmed to me that Robert is the most capable and effective person I know. Robert is serving in one of the most difficult places in one of the most innovative ways with very few resources. I support him very strongly and sell the opportunity to my friends.

"Now we've got a goal to give even more. As we give to Robert's work, it feels like God keeps stretching [our goal], and then He keeps making it possible for us to give more. Then the next year something else feels like a stretch. He's the one who's the giver.

"And through our relationship with Robert, God has made us care about India and about Robert's work there, and it's become part of the fabric of our family."

The more we understand God and His heart, the more we understand His passions. "The things of earth will grow strangely dim in the light of His glory and grace," as Helen Lemmel wrote in the hymn "Turn Your Eyes upon Jesus."

FOLLOW YOUR HEART? NO, ASK FOR A NEW HEART

I have a shelf full of books about giving. Most of these start with "find your giving passion." Many secular, well-meaning advisors encourage readers to look within to find out what causes and programs they, personally, are drawn to. And many Christians have borrowed this concept of inside-out giving. They all say some version of "look to your own passions."

But there is a more excellent and joy-filled way to give! The God of the universe wants to *give* you passions. The greatest joy comes when we look to our Father instead of ourselves, hear what He's excited about, and then act on it.

God has given us all different strengths and interests and giving personalities. All of our God-given uniqueness finds expression in the vast playground of God's passions. But starting with our own passions can lead us astray.

For example, I've loved American football for as long as I can remember. So I may ask, "How can I give in a way that expresses my longstanding passion for football?" Perhaps I find youth leagues in urban areas that need support. Perhaps I provide football equipment to my local school. Perhaps I give to my college to help our football team build a better facility or hire better coaches.

Have I used God's money well? After all, He gave me this passion for football, and He gave me this money. But basing my giving on a love for football doesn't necessarily bring Him a Kingdom return.

My passion for Xbox or cooking may be good. But building my generosity around video games or the perfect grilled steak may lead me off course. These might be silly examples, but you don't have to look far to find wealthy people who have built organizational monuments to their personal passions.

Remember to ask good, big questions. Start with "God, what is your passion? What did You devote your time to on earth? What do You want us to do?"

The process needs to start with Him, but often *His* passions will lead us back to our *own* passions. If I love sports, I may find ministries that use sports to reach people with the Gospel. If I love the life of the mind, perhaps there's an organization that uses the classics to create conversations about the Gospel with intellectuals.

My dad is amazing at building, and he's able to use that gift—and his generosity—to help ministries build homes for those in need, spreading the Gospel as they go. If you're passionate about cars, you may find church-based ministries that fix up old cars and give them to single moms. Within God's purposes, you can find amazing ways to put your passions to use. But it starts with Him.

WHEN GOD GIVES US HIS PASSIONS

For most us, the deepest joy in giving comes when God reveals something better than we would have. Our family was not passionate about children in the Himalayas until God introduced us to Robert, who runs Gospel-centered schools and medical clinics there. We didn't even know about the Oromo region of Ethiopia until we met a man who serves there. We had no special passion for new churches in Peru. But when we saw the needs of people building shacks on a hillside outside of Lima, people who had no place to worship and no pastor ministering to them, God stirred our hearts. His passion became ours.

God gave us His passions. He taught us to invest in what He cares about. When we listened at His feet, our hearts changed and became larger and more connected to His.

What is God passionate about?

This is important. When you give, He's passionate *first* about your own discipleship. He doesn't need your money. But beyond that, there are three passages in Scripture in which Jesus gives us a window into His priorities.

In Matthew 22, someone asks Jesus what the greatest commandment is. Jesus answers:

> *You shall love the Lord your God with all your heart and with all your soul and with all your mind. This*

*is the great and first commandment. And a second is
like it: You shall love your neighbor as yourself. On
these two commandments depend all the Law and
the Prophets.* (Matthew 22:37-39)

Love God. Love people. Everything depends on that.

He also, in His last words on earth, talks about growing the
family of people who worship Him:

*Go...and make disciples of all nations, baptizing
them in the name of the Father and of the Son and
of the Holy Spirit, teaching them to observe all that I
have commanded you.* (Matthew 28:19-20)

Christians across the centuries have called these passages
the Great Commandment and the Great Commission. These
are the center of His heart.

God's heart is large enough to encompass every cause, but
they all lead back to these three concepts: love God, love people,
and make disciples. This has been our legacy as Christians
from the beginning of the church, when the twelve disciples
cared for widows, prayed, and preached the word (Acts 6:1-7).

God's passion is still for us to pray (loving Him), care for
tangible needs (loving people), and preach the word (making
disciples).

LOVE GOD, LOVE PEOPLE, MAKE DISCIPLES

The Great Commandment and the Great Commission go together. As we "love the Lord your God," we end up making disciples. As we make disciples and teach them, we "love your neighbor as yourself" (Matthew 22:37, 39). Loving God leads us to love our neighbors. The best way to love our neighbors is to show them how to love God. It's a beautiful, virtuous cycle.

Some givers emphasize making disciples—spreading the Gospel and ensuring that people have Bibles. They look to the Great Commission. Other givers feel more compelled by meeting material physical needs. They look to Jesus's teaching about the sheep and the goats in Matthew 25, pointing out that "whatever you did for one of the least of these brothers and sisters of mine, you did for me" (Matthew 25:40, NIV).

An African church planter gave me a way to think about this holistically. We sat at an outdoor café in a mountain village, enjoying a cultural meal. I asked him how these two concepts—making disciples and loving people—fit together. Here's what he said:

> "There is an area not far from here that used to have no Christians. It was dangerous, and there were few jobs. The government would not allow foreigners to go there. Then we began planting churches there and found a great harvest. It changed the whole

culture. It's not that everyone became Christian. But enough people became Christian that it changed everything. It changed the way that women are treated. It changed the poverty because people started to share and trust each other and became more honest in business. It changed the way poor people are treated since we believe everyone is made in the image of God. Without the Gospel, no other force can change that. The church changes that. Now the government allows people to travel there. There are still wicked people, but they are outnumbered."

The Great Commandment and the Great Commission are the same. The best way to love people is to make disciples. And the best way to make disciples is to love people. These priorities will shape *what* we give to and they'll also shape *how* we give.

LOVING GOD IN *WHAT YOU GIVE TO*

In order to love God as we give, we need to focus on God's purposes. As we've seen, the money isn't ours; it's His. We show our love for Him when we desire what He desires, when we give to causes that glorify Him.

If that feels abstract, it's OK. We can look to the early church for examples. The closer we get to the fountainhead—the place from which the church's river begins—the more likely we are to find pure, clean water, untainted by the polluted tributaries of the world's culture. In Chapter 6 of this book, we'll take a deeper look at the causes that our earliest brothers and sisters supported.

For now, just recognize that whatever ministries you give to, God should be at the center.

LOVING PEOPLE IN *WHAT YOU GIVE TO*

Many Christians wonder whether it's OK to give to friends who need help, or to ministries that focus primarily on meeting material needs like food and clothing rather than spiritual needs like evangelism and discipleship. Of course!

Giving is a wonderful way to fulfill Jesus's Great Commandment to love our neighbors as we love ourselves. Saif in Dubai says, "When the blind man came to Jesus, he felt his utmost need was to see, so Jesus healed his sight and that led him to faith. Just like that, I can say to a family I know, 'I'll buy you a month's worth of groceries.'"

In China, Jiang does something similar. "If the brothers or sisters at church really have needs, we discuss what we can provide. We give help and give what we have to other people."

In my own life, not long ago, the son of a friend at church needed some medical testing. The child had symptoms of ADHD, but the test to confirm the diagnosis was fairly expensive and their health insurance wouldn't cover it. My friend mentioned the amount they needed. Carolyn and I asked the Lord about it and felt a peace about covering it. The boy had the test, which led his doctors to put him on medication that changed his entire life. His parents were grateful that God allowed us to use His money to help this boy. They felt supported, loved, and seen by God. Our relationship deepened, and both families' joy in God grew.

Sometimes we give to see others become followers of Jesus, and sometimes we give because *we* are followers of Jesus.

"It's a complex Kingdom that God's building," says my friend Tom in Australia, "but He's got it all covered."

MAKING DISCIPLES IN *WHAT YOU GIVE TO*

I love God, and I love people. I have no greater joy in giving than when I can connect the God I love to people I love. It's the greatest gift I can give.

In my conversations, I've found that Christians outside the West are more attuned to seeing spiritual needs as paramount. Amit in India speaks for dozens of givers I've talked with when he says, "I believe that the spiritual is more important than the material need. I believe ministries I support should focus on the needs of eternity. Even if they're good at doing charitable work, if there's not attention to eternity, we stay away from that."

If a person's giving doesn't somehow point people to Jesus, it doesn't solve a problem; it merely postpones the problem.

We can give the homeless person a home *forever* in heaven. We can slake thirst *forever* with living water. To the sick, we can offer perfectly functioning bodies *forever* in heaven. To the uneducated, we can offer the chance to learn more of God *forever* in heaven. To the oppressed, we can offer the chance to rule with God *forever* in heaven. To the prisoner, we can give freedom *forever* in heaven. Focusing on spiritual needs doesn't mean that we're ignoring immediate needs, but we are approaching them more holistically.

Alex in the United Kingdom says, "I see so many otherwise mature Christian people not thinking about how to give. It pains me when they don't focus on Word ministry. They put their money where the secular dollar can do its work."

Many givers tell us that their country thrives when the church thrives, so they invest disproportionately in church planting and training church leaders. In God's beautiful economy, spreading the Gospel spreads healing. When people come to Christ and start loving one another as He does, physical *and* spiritual needs are met. Our giving to the Great Commandment points people toward the Gospel; the Gospel, when it takes root, helps fulfill the Great Commandment.

All of our giving should, in some way, point people toward heaven.

Now we come to a critical thing to understand. God wants us to do these three things—love God, love people, make disciples—not just *in* our giving, but *as* we give and in the *ways* we give. He doesn't just care about your money's destination; He cares about its journey.

We need to follow His priorities both in *where* we give and *how* we give.

Paul puts it much better in 1 Corinthians 13:3 (NIV): "If I give all I possess to the poor… but do not have love, I gain nothing."

LOVING GOD, LOVING PEOPLE, AND MAKING DISCIPLES IN *THE WAY* WE GIVE

Giving is a great chance for us to draw near to our Father. We get to reflect on the words of Jesus, listen to His Spirt, and ask Him what He wants us to do with His money. The whole process builds intimacy. This is what it means to love God in the way we give.

It's like you're going on an adventure with your dad. God wants to take you on a fishing trip. The point isn't to get as many fish as you can—you could do that at the supermarket. The point is to share an adventure and a connection.

We can also love people in the way we give. I've talked to a few givers who shared that they used to be a bit *too* strategic, with rigid parameters governing how they deployed each gift. But many of them found that part of following the Great Commandment is loving the people close to them. Now they set aside small amounts—perhaps 5 or 10 percent of their total giving—to support causes that matter to their friends and build relationships.

They do this even if specific projects don't seem to make objective sense or don't bring the highest Kingdom return. I've certainly been in that situation. But if a cause matters to a person I care about, why not show them I love them by giving? Why not attend a banquet with a friend or help the local school's fundraiser? It's all part of loving my neighbors.

The Great Commandment and the Great Commission don't just guide us to the right causes; they also guide the way that we express generosity.

We can make disciples *as* we give by bringing others along and discipling them in the grace of giving—an area often neglected in traditional discipleship programs.

Tom in Australia is part of a group of givers focused on church planting. He says, "There are people in the group I lead who are very busy in their businesses. So we sit back and think about giving. We start with biblical teaching about giving. We give together, but the only point is that we gather in one place at one time."

Can you hear the discipleship happening? Tom is making disciples *as* he gives, through the *way* he gives.

As we align ourselves with God's passions and give to the things He's passionate about, we find joy giving. But your Father doesn't just want to hand you a list of His passions and send you out with His checkbook. He wants you to talk with Him about how to walk within His priorities. That leads us to prayer.

5: PRAYER

Hearing the Owner's Heart

LUCY IN CHINA WAS a new Christian and a new giver. She hadn't heard much about the theology of giving, or about theology at all. Lucy had never, in fact, given *anything* to anyone outside her family.

Then she attended a Journey of Generosity event that we held in Guangzhou, and she learned about asking God how much to give and where to give. So she did.

Lucy owns a chain of kindergartens. In a culture that emphasizes education the way China does, great kindergartens are big business. When Lucy prayed, God revealed to her that she should give away all the profits of one of her kindergartens, which was the equivalent of about $150,000. That's quite a bit bigger than the first gift I ever gave!

Lucy wondered where to give the money, so she prayed. She asked God, "What do You want me to do with this money that You've given me?"

Lucy says, "God then gave me a three-point strategy for giving." She gave one-third to a prayer ministry, one-third to a workplace ministry in China, and one-third to the organization that introduced her to the message of biblical generosity.

In response to Lucy's big open-ended questions, God provided clear answers. And those answers brought Lucy joy and peace in her giving.

WHAT DOES GOD WANT ME TO GIVE TO?

In my email inbox right now is a message from Harold in Australia, asking, "What does God want me to give to? Should I be giving to what I resonate with or keep more open to where God wants me to give?"

In the coming days and weeks, Harold and I will have a conversation in which I'll ask him questions about his life, about how he connects with God, and about how God speaks to him.

Harold—and all of us—generally fall into one of three categories:

1. Listening to God is new to me.

2. I listen to God, but not about money and giving.

3. I listen to God about money and giving.

Hopefully, we are all moving toward category 3, but some Christians doubt that they can directly hear from God. They know God is actively involved in the world around them, but their experience or tradition makes them doubt that they can hear Him. The testimonies from the givers I've met around the world, however, are consistent: our Father speaks to us about our giving. We all speak to different people in different ways at different times, and God does the same. Some people hear specific words and phrases from Him, while others see pictures or receive dreams. For some, listening to God is more about waiting for the Spirit to give a sense of peace. They'll say, "God gave me peace about going in this direction" or "I just didn't feel at ease with doing that." Elijah heard a "still small voice" (1 Kings 19:12, NKJV). Peter had a vision (Acts 10:10-16), Paul heard a voice (Acts 9) and Cornelius saw an angel (Acts 10:5)..

My wife, Carolyn, serves as a prayer counselor. She encourages people to ask specific parts of the Trinity specific questions. "Father, why do you love me?" "Holy Spirit, why am I feeling this anxiety about this issue?" Then she and her counselee listen for the answer and obey in faith. Of course God will never contradict Scripture. But our Father loves to speak to us personally, and to waken and open our ears to His voice (Isaiah 50:4-5).

QUESTIONS TO ASK GOD ABOUT MONEY AND GIVING

In my conversations with givers around the world, I've asked about how they pray. Here are some words and phrases they used:

- "Lord, I want to please you and not man. Help me to quiet these voices that urge me to want attention or to get credit. Please help me to have pure motives. Please quiet my soul."

- "God, what do you want us to do with this money that you have generated?"

- "God, how can I allow you space to move in my heart? How can I give you more control?"

- "Holy Spirit, convict me about what to do. Make my giving consistent with your Word."

- "God, *how* should I pray about this issue?"

Each child of God will have a slightly different way of talking to their Father about money and giving. But He calls each of us to ask Him for wisdom and to then listen quietly for an answer.

Simon, a businessman in the United Kingdom, receives numerous letters asking for gifts. He used to lay the letters out on a table and ask God to lead him to the right ones. Over the years, he's changed his approach. He now asks God to guide his overall giving strategy and then finds causes that fit that strategy, while leaving room for spontaneous giving opportunities.

Your Father loves to give you wisdom when you ask Him in faith. James says, "If any of you lacks wisdom, let him ask God, who gives generously to all without reproach, and it will be given him" (James 1:5).

Scripture tells us over and over to be discerning and thoughtful as we pursue God's wisdom. "Ponder the path of your feet; then all your ways will be sure" (Proverbs 4:26). When He gives us this wisdom and renews our minds, we can "discern what is the will of God, what is good and acceptable and perfect" (Romans 12:2).

How do we know that what we're hearing is God's wisdom and not our own thoughts? James provides the secret code when he shows us to ask if the answer is "first pure, then peaceable, gentle, open to reason, full of mercy and good fruits, impartial and sincere." (James 3:17). If so, then it is His wisdom and not ours.

Methodist Church founder John Wesley led a "Holy Club" in the mid-eighteenth century. Among other pursuits, the group had a list of twenty-two accountability questions they asked one another. One of my favorites is "Do I pray about the money I spend?"

Spending money is an opportunity to reconnect with our Father. Each time we pull out our credit card or checkbook, it is an opportunity to ask, "Is this what You want me to do with Your money?" If the answer is yes, the Father gives us peace.

But on many occasions when I was about to pay for something, I asked the Lord and heard a "no." For example, I was recently on the verge of buying tickets to a music festival for Carolyn's birthday. The price was high. Was Carolyn worth it to me? Of course. But somehow, when I checked with the Owner, it didn't seem that He wanted me to give that specific gift right then.

This prayer-led process brings peace. When we ask the Owner and feel the peace, then we can move ahead with confidence that God has given us a gift. We can receive it with gratitude and without guilt.

ASK GOD PROACTIVELY AND RESPOND WHEN HE NUDGES

Most givers I know emphasize the importance of developing a Spirit-led plan. We are to "try to discern what is pleasing to the Lord" (Ephesians 5:10), using the tools He gives us. We should all be asking Him, "God, what do you want me to do here?" And, whether we ask or not, we should all be ready to obey when He prompts us.

Sometimes, God will put a specific need in front of us and prompt us to do something about it. For one friend, that meant giving away her couch. She sensed God's leading and obeyed.

Not long ago, I spoke with Hassem, who has very modest income. Hassem had received an unexpected windfall and began to plan how to use it. His wife had a dream in which God showed her that they should give away the money and even showed her who should receive it. When she told her husband, Hassem jokingly suggested that she go back to sleep and have a different dream. But as he prayed, Hassem realized that his wife's dream was from God, so they gave away the money, even adding a little extra of their own.

We should all leave space for this kind of spontaneous giving. On average, givers with whom I spoke leave 5 to 10 percent of their giving for spontaneous needs that God brings to them; the interviewee with the highest "spontaneous" percentage holds 50 percent for these kinds of gifts. As these needs arise, they follow the admonition in 2 Corinthians 9:7 not to give "under compulsion," and so they take some time—usually a day—to pray before acting.

GIVING PLANS

Many of the most thoughtful and intentional givers I've talked with have established giving plans. These plans vary in their structures but usually include these elements:

Purpose of our giving
How much we give
Values that guide our giving
Projects, places, or people to whom we give

For example, a giver in the US has decided to give more than 60 percent locally and more than 25 percent globally. An Australian has allocated this way:

- Christian media (20%)

- Church plants/growth (18%)

- Youth work (18%)

- Evangelism (7%)

- Other (37%)

One giver set a rule that they do not want to be the sole provider of more than 15 percent of their church's budget. Another has decided not to support building projects.

Their specifics will not be your specifics, but each of these givers spent focused, proactive time asking God, consulting with others, praying as a family, and then establishing some God-given parameters for their giving.

At Generosity Path, we have developed a twenty-four-hour retreat during which families or individuals can work through a Spirit-led listening process, emerging with a draft giving plan. We call this Next Steps.[3]

PRAYING THE PARABLE OF THE TALENTS

Toward the end of His ministry, Jesus told the unforgettable parable of the talents.

A wealthy man gives his servants five talents, two talents, and one talent. The first two servants "went at once and traded with them" and doubled their investments. The last one "hid his master's money." The owner rewarded the first two but called the last one "wicked and slothful." The last servant should have "invested my money with the bankers, and at my coming I should have received what was my own with interest" (Matthew 25:14-30).

Scholars tell us that a talent was worth about 20 years' worth of wages. The median income in the United States is a bit over $50,000. The servant entrusted with just one talent, then, is handling $1 million.

When talking with givers, my colleague Lee Behar asks, "Why does Jesus tell a story about investing a *huge* amount of money? His followers didn't have much money." Lee believes that Jesus may have been speaking to *us* even more than He was speaking to *them*.

---

3   To host a Next Steps session, visit www.GenerosityPath.org/gatherings.

In the story, the owner wants his servants to invest his wealth in order to bring a return. The lesson we see in that is that when our Master entrusts us with resources, our task is to work to grow them and to deliver returns. The glorious news, of course, is that God is involved in the return. Still, it's up to us to step out in faith, deploying His resources wisely and praying diligently.

Jesus details the rewards He gives to those who invest well and the consequences allotted to those who don't. The master rewarded those who delivered returns with more responsibility and the "joy of your master" (Matthew 25:21, 23). He punished the one who did not deliver, taking what little he had and casting him "into the outer darkness" (Matthew 23:30).

It's a harrowing story. What a blessing that we get to be the effective servants and enter into His joy! This makes me want to keep praying, asking Him questions to ensure that I'm investing in His ways.

Lee draws three lessons from this story:

1. The Owner Is Interested in Results

God, what results do You hope come from the resources You've entrusted to me?

No matter how we invest our resources, our Master wants us not to bury the resources He gives us or to play it safe. Jesus promises the "joy of your master" to those who faithfully deploy

His resources. He leads us to ask, "Father, what do you want with these resources?"

Throughout Scripture, we see that God gives with great generosity. Jesus was rich and "for your sake he became poor, so that you by his poverty might become rich" (2 Corinthians 8:9). He loves to give good gifts to His children. He adopts us and gives us a place in His family and at His table.

But it does not end there. Once He's enriched us spiritually and financially, He tells us to share those riches with others. He gives us comfort that pours out to comfort others. He laid down His life for us, so we lay down our lives for others. Because He lives, we will live. Because He loves us, we love others. And because He gives us "the world's goods" (1 John 3:17), we give away the world's goods as we see needs.

In each case, He shares generously, but He also loves when we steward His generosity well. That's His way.

Vlad in central Europe says, "Strategic giving is to deploy limited resources to the projects or activities that can bring the biggest impact for the Kingdom. Many people don't think like that. They say, 'I know some church around me or some ministry.' I've found that as I think more strategically and encourage my friends to think more strategically, we have wiser giving, and we increase giving because people like that it's strategic and thoughtful."

God gives us gifts: our time, our families, our funds, our abilities. He gently reminds us that " you are not your own, for you were bought with a price" (1 Corinthians 6:19-20). And if we are not our own, then we need His wisdom on how to use what He's given us. Paul tells us to "look carefully then how you walk, not as unwise but as wise, making the best use of the time, because the days are evil. Therefore do not be foolish, but understand what the will of the Lord is" (Ephesians 5:15-17).

The good news is that when He assigns us to be stewards, He provides the means—through the Spirit—to fulfill our role as stewards. Let's let the Spirit lead us to invest His money in His way.

2. We Need Others to Bring Returns

"God, with whom do You want me investing Your resources?

In the parable, the master wants the servants to rely on others to help bring returns. He says that the wicked servant should have invested his talent with "bankers."

To bring Kingdom returns, involve a group with expertise, positioned to bring returns on what you invest. This kind of giving is more than one person can accomplish alone—and that's God's good design.

Johan in the Netherlands says, "You need to find expertise. Too many wealthy people think that because they were good at making money, they're good at giving money. No. You need to hire people to study the market, develop strategies. Be a bit more professional. Don't just go for the people you happen to know."

Many people who have much to give try to start their own institutes or develop a charity that meets their particular passion instead of turning to those who are already experienced and in the field. Too often, they are surrounded by a group of acolytes whose paychecks depend on the wealthy person and who, therefore, are afraid to question their boss' decisions. Millions of dollars are wasted annually on these personal passion projects.

Friends who work at the wonderful ministry Young Life report that every week, one or two people approach them to try to donate or sell their land for Young Life to use as a camp. There's no shortage of Christian camps, but evidently many people think the world needs one more. Meanwhile, dozens of other camps fall into disrepair for lack of resources.

We all have blind spots, and we rely on others to help us see them. The landowners have a passion for their own properties and their visions for how it could be used. But others could help them see the property as a resource that could be liquidated and used to fund great Kingdom work.

Then there is the example I heard about the man who bought a farm so he could invite Christian artists to come and collaborate together. The cost to purchase, fix up, and operate the farm ran into millions of dollars. His staff told me that he could have just rented another farm or available retreat center, likely saving millions of dollars while achieving the same results. By going it alone, this giver missed the chance to build community, to partner with others who share his passions, and to experience joy and sorrow together.

Creating community around shared passions is beautiful. We sharpen each other's ideas, correct each other's thinking, and find accountability. But if you cannot find others who believe in the vision for a self-funded passion project, that may be a sign.

Here are a few questions to help givers discern the difference between "passion projects" and "God projects":

- Is this ultimately your project or God's project?

- If someone else were doing a similar project, would that threaten you or thrill you?

- Do your projects involve people who can be objective?

- Are you open to having others fund this with you? If not, why not?

- When God does something great in the project, will you get to celebrate with others what God did, or will you be seen as bragging about what you did?

When we involve others, we find accountability. Let's be clear: people we pay are rarely the best people to give us accountability. Instead, follow Jesus's advice and invest with the "bankers." Find the people who have expertise, partner with them, and support them.

3. The Owner Encourages Taking Some Risks

God, what are the risks You want me to take with the resources You've entrusted to me?

The final thing we see in the parable of the talents is that investing in pursuit of Kingdom results involves risk. We don't need to worry that we find the perfect opportunity, but we must identify an opportunity that is likely to have great impact.

Generous Christian givers are eager to go on adventures, to risk more, and to see what God does.

Johan from the Netherlands has found that "we need to treat giving more like venture capital. Too many people, especially those who inherit money, are too risk averse."

Some givers focus on the wrong metrics. Many people, for example, support digging wells in the developing world. Who doesn't want to dig a well for a village that doesn't have water? That's great! But experts have found that one-third of these new wells are inoperable at any given time. It's fun to dig a new well; it's hard to invest in maintenance. Yet most water charities focus on new wells because givers want the quick win—the well they can see and visit.

The Economist wrote about givers who overemphasize outcomes: "Demanding proof of impact may push charities to focus on short-term outcomes, rather than more meaningful long-term measures of success… 'What you don't want is all charities gravitating towards the easier projects that guarantee high levels of success'" ("Doing Good by Doing Well," *The Economist,* May 21, 2015, https://www.economist.com/news/international/21651815-lessons-business-charities-doing-good-doing-well).

Secular philanthropists struggle to be patient, but the wisest are learning to do so. How much *more* patient should Christian givers be as we wait for eternal results? After prayer and discernment, God may lead you toward projects that are higher risk but will have greater impact in eternity.

Ian from the Philippines says, "As a philanthropist, I didn't want to be one of those Christians who had been given talents and put them under a rock. I wanted to do more. When I found out what God could do with my money through Campus Crusade for Christ, I felt like God had thrown me a life preserver."

"I'm not in favor of perpetuating institutions from the Victorian age," says Lewis from the United Kingdom. "They do good work, but what about something that's new, innovative, cutting edge? Where is today's solution?"

A Christian foundation in California says that it prefers to pursue projects that may be too risky for others. But this raises a question: What *kinds* of risks are we supposed to be taking? How do we know when to "bet" in order to turn the Master's talents into more?

Using these three questions, we can pray the Parable of the Talents, ensuring that we are in step with the Owner's wishes.

> *God, what results do You hope come from the resources You've entrusted to me?*
>
> *God, with whom do You want me investing Your resources?*
>
> *God, what are the risks You want me to take with the resources You've entrusted to me?*

As we learn what God is passionate about and pray for specific guidance, God will give us windows into His heart.

Another way to better understand His heart is to see how His earliest followers invested *their* talents. What did *they* give to? And what does that mean for our giving? How did they experience joy giving? We look at their giving priorities in the next chapter.

6: PRIORITIES
Pastors, Proclamation, and Poverty

PETR AND HIS FAMILY in the Czech Republic sold their business and suddenly had a tremendous amount to give away. He had built the company by following God's leading and working methodically. "Why should my giving be different?" he asked.

"By praying and asking God to show us, He helped us focus and set principles of our giving. We want the greatest Kingdom impact. We want to be Great Commission givers, but where? We asked God and ourselves 'what are the most strategic mission fields in the world nowadays?' Having that focus in our giving helps grow our expertise. We can connect with ministries in this area and be better-educated givers."

Givers like Petr ask the critical question *How do I decide where to give?*

Across the centuries, the early Christians speak to us through Scripture, telling us what they did. And what we find when we start to listen is that the early church gave the most to... themselves.

Physical needs surrounded our brothers and sisters. The first century had its share of the blind, the sick, the poor, the widows, the orphans, the lepers, the lame, the deaf, and the foreigners. Yet even among this cacophony of needs, when we survey the New Testament we see the earliest Christians giving to just three causes: the church, the spread of the Gospel, and those in need in their church family.

Does this mean that we should only give to these three things? Not necessarily. But it's a helpful starting point. We don't need to follow the early church's example mechanically, but we'd be silly not to try to learn from those who were closest to Jesus in time and space.

GIVING TO THE LOCAL CHURCH

As you consider where you are called to give, start with those who feed your own soul. Here's how Paul says it in Galatians 6:6 (NIV): "The one who receives instruction in the word should share all good things with their instructor."

Have you ever thought about the people whose giving led *you* to meet Jesus? When we focus too much on ourselves as givers, it's easy to forget the humbling truth that we are also receivers.

I became a Christian at a small church in Oregon that my uncle pastored. The givers to that church were instrumental, then, in my journey toward Jesus. My faith continued to grow at summer camps, youth groups, and through college ministry leaders. Each of their givers impacted my journey in some way.

Paul encouraged the church to pay elders with "double honor, especially those who labor in preaching and teaching. For the Scripture says, 'You shall not muzzle an ox when it treads out the grain,' and, 'The laborer deserves his wages.'" (1 Timothy 5:17-18).

Those who sow "spiritual things among you…reap material things from you" (1 Corinthians 9:11) because "the Lord commanded that those who proclaim the gospel should get their living by the gospel" (1 Corinthians 9:14).

Who paid local pastors in Paul's time? Their local churches. And that's still the case today. Generous givers around the world keep their local church at the center of their giving. Many set aside the first 10 percent of their income to give to their church and then give what is above and beyond that to other ministries they're called to support. Those with extreme wealth with whom I spoke tend to set aside about one-third of their total *giving* (not their total income) to their local church.

We have an incredible opportunity to support the ministries that have had significant impacts on our families and our personal walks with Jesus. We can give to support the work of an author or podcast preacher who affected us. What an opportunity for blessing!

Yet often, when I talk to Christians around the world, I hear a surprising piece of feedback: church giving is not fun. The impression is that we don't get to control where our giving goes within the church, and we receive fewer reports on what happens with the funds. There usually aren't fundraising professionals whose job it is to thank us, send us stories of impact, or generally make a big deal about us and our giving. At most, we get a year-end receipt.

Local church giving means submitting ourselves to our church's leadership. For wealthy people who are seldom told "no," this submission can be uncomfortable and unusual. However, it's also healthy, helpful, and, most of all, biblical.

But our giving does not stop at our local church doors. Joy-filled global givers also focus their giving through the church or in ways that have a local church component. Scripture shows us to prioritize gifts that have a connection to a local church. Giver after giver said, "The local church is the hope of the world" or "God's work happens through the local church."

Li in China explains, "Giving in China is through your local church. There was a massive flood a couple of years ago in Southwest China. The house church movement, which is technically illegal, raised quite a significant sum of money. We took the money to the official government and said, 'Here is our gift to people in trouble. This is from the house church movement.'"

So today, if we're looking at a water project or community development project, we can ensure that our gift is connected to a church in that region.

Steve Corbett and Brian Fikkert, the authors of *When Helping Hurts: How to Alleviate Poverty Without Hurting the Poor...and Yourself*, encourage givers to ensure that the causes they support are connected to the local church. "Whenever God's people choose to minister outside the direct oversight of the local church, they should always be seeking to partner with the local church, which has God-given authority over people's spiritual lives."

GIVING TO SPREAD THE GOSPEL

One of the early church's chief expenses was supporting those who proclaimed the Gospel. Paul says in Romans 10:

> For "everyone who calls on the name of the Lord will be saved." How then will they call on him in whom they have not believed? And how are they to believe in him of whom they have never heard? And how are

they to hear without someone preaching? And how are they to preach unless they are sent? (Romans 10:13-15)

The churches responded to Paul's call. Early Christians planted new churches, sent missionaries, and proclaimed Christ. Givers in Luke 8 supported Jesus's own teaching and healing ministry. Theophilus underwrote the cost of preparing the books of Luke and Acts. Phoebe, the Philippians, and numerous hosts made Paul's missionary journeys possible.

The early church rose to the challenge, and because they did, *you* have a relationship with Jesus today. And many Christians around the world today are committed to passing the Gospel on to others:

- "As a Christian, I should focus on the cause of Christ. I try to give mainly to evangelization, spreading the Gospel." (Hungary)

- "Christians here are deeply committed to world mission through church planting. We may give some to the poor, to orphans, widows, to sex trafficking, but mostly evangelism." (Korea)

- "The challenge for us is to think about the *best* use of money. We've decided that it's giving to strategic Gospel causes. Gospel giving is key!" (Australia)

- "We sow into missions. This is a mission field.
  We need to step up to see people saved." (Dubai)

In many parts of the world, the Gospel is arriving for the first time. Most Christians I meet in China have known Christ for just three or four years. These new believers are passionate about spreading the Good News and enthusiastically support programs that bring Jesus to even more people. It sounds a lot like the early church.

Sometimes we give to see the Kingdom come to others, and sometimes we give because the Kingdom has come to *us*. That brings us to the final way the early church gave.

GIVING TO THE NEEDY WE ENCOUNTER

Giving to those with needs is a hallmark of the New Testament. In the parables of the Good Samaritan (Luke 10:25-37) and the story of the wedding banquet (Luke 14:15-24), Jesus calls us to give to those at the margins. And His early church prioritized caring for the poor. When Paul receives the blessing of the early apostles for his ministry to the Gentiles, he does so with one proviso: "Only, they asked us to remember the poor, the very thing I was eager to do" (Galatians 2:10). So remembering the poor is an essential part of our faith.

But which poor? For Christian givers today, there are needs all over the world—in developing countries, among the homeless, in the inner cities, and beyond. Where do we start?

Scripture could have us find the neediest person and give to them. Or Scripture could have us find the most efficient ministry and fund that. But Scripture offers a different way.

The way that the New Testament tells us to give is messy, relational, and challenging. Jesus asks us to invest *ourselves* before we invest our money. It's a lot more than just writing some checks.

Giving starts with the people you see: first your own family; and then His family, the church; and then everyone else. Think of three concentric circles:

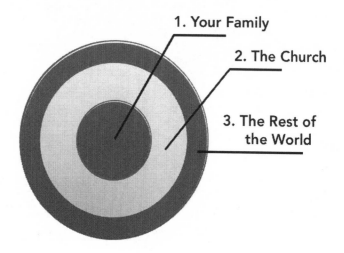

1. Your Family

2. The Church

3. The Rest of the World

As we look more deeply, remember that it's a matter of degree, not decree. God will bring you all kinds of opportunities to be generous. Ask Him what He wants.

Circle 1: Family First

This one is straightforward. Paul writes, "if anyone does not provide for his relatives, and especially for members of his household, he has denied the faith and is worse than an unbeliever" (1 Timothy 5:8). Biblical giving begins with your heart and your home, and when we decide to give away money and goods, the Bible teaches that we should begin with those closest to us: our families.

Many cultures around the world take this to an extreme, giving so much to their families and extended families that they have little left to give to other Kingdom causes.

Park in Korea says, "We give money to our parents. This is Korean culture, so 20 to 30 percent of monthly income goes to parents. Before asking someone to give more in Korea, one needs to understand their extended family's needs."

Jeong, who also lives in Korea, agrees. "I tell people that in many situations, they should give money to their parents, if their parents are poor, and not to the church. Giving and tithing needs to be balanced with giving money to your parents."

Circle 2: Treat Your Church Like Family

Once we ensure our families are cared for, we turn to the needs of the local church. "But if anyone has the world's goods and sees his brother in need, yet closes his heart against him, how does God's love abide in him?" (1 John 3:17).

Remember that "brother" in the New Testament is not the same as "neighbor." Scripture is consistent and clear: our priority should be the family of God. The lawyer asked Jesus, "Who is my neighbor?" and Jesus told him the Samaritan was a neighbor (Luke 10:29-37). But "brother" refers to the church, the family of God, the "children of God." Jesus says in Matthew 12:50 (NIV), "Whoever does the will of my Father in heaven is my brother...."

Givers around the world, especially those in countries where they are in the minority as Christians, are great at caring for their spiritual families. Wu from China says, "In addition to our tithe, we try to be generous to our [Christian] brothers and sisters. If we know someone in need, we are glad to give to spiritual siblings and to needs of people in the church."

In Beijing, giving at one particular church was not going well. Keung had just become an elder and wanted to take the pulse of the church on giving. He met church members for tea and asked, "So are you excited about giving to our church?" Person after person said, "Why should we give to the church when they don't have a need and they're not giving to the community?"

Keung looked into it and realized that the church had accumulated more than $1 million. The church wasn't a conduit for giving; it had become a reservoir. Keung prayed and then made a proposal. "We need to change," he said to the church's leaders, "and it starts with us. Let's ask God how we can do what we're asking people to do. Let's be sacrificial *as leaders* and sacrificial *as a church*."

The elders agreed. They spent the church's surplus funds caring for the needs of the community. They gave to widows, orphans, the elderly, the homeless, and refugees. They filmed their giving, bringing the joyful reports back to the congregation Sunday after Sunday. After months of these generous acts, they asked the congregation to respond.

The people loved the way the church now handled its money, and they gave another full $1 million.

People love giving to churches that are conduits; they don't love giving to churches that are mere bank accounts. When the church radically cares for its own, believers flourish, and we have even more to give to those outside our walls. As others extend generosity to new believers, meeting their physical and spiritual needs, the new believers turn around and look for ways to pour into others. That's the economy of the Kingdom.

Paul emphasizes the importance of starting with the family of faith. In Galatians 6, he writes: "So then, as we have opportunity, let us do good to everyone, and especially to those who are of the household of faith" (Galatians 6:10).

Nicolas from France says, "We have emphasized too much helping everyone and not focused enough on giving to brothers and sisters in the faith. I emphasize taking care of other Christians."

Preferring to give to Christians strikes some skeptics as less generous. "Oh, so I can't give anything to non-Christians?" But that's not what Scripture says. Paul says give to everyone, but *especially* to those "who are of the household of faith." In other words, give to Christians.

James, the brother of Jesus, agrees. "If a brother or sister is poorly clothed and lacking in daily food, and one of you says to them, 'Go in peace, be warmed and filled,' without giving them the things needed for the body, what good is that?'" (James 2:15-16).

Does God want us to prefer the needs of believers rather than the needs of the rest of the world? It seems He does.

Consider the example from Matthew 10, the passage that inspires so many Christians to talk about ministry as giving a "cup of cold water" to the needy. Jesus goes out of his way to encourage us to give to one another *because* we are part of the same family, saying, "Whoever gives one of these little ones even a cup of cold water *because he is a disciple*, truly I say to you, he will by no means lose his reward" (Matthew 10:42; emphasis added).

A generation later, Paul wrote to the Romans, one of the wealthiest churches. They lived in the most powerful city in the history of the world. Some even lived in Caesar's household. Yet Paul doesn't tell them to send their affluence to meet general needs. No, he tells them to "contribute to the needs *of the saints*" (Romans 12:13; emphasis added).

In Acts 11, Agabus predicts a famine that would impact the whole Roman world. The disciples decide to take up a collection. "The disciples, as each one was able, decided to provide help for the *brothers and sisters* living in Judea" (Acts 11:29, NIV; emphasis added).

The Macedonian church desired to help "in the relief of the saints" (2 Corinthians 8:4). Paul says to "share with the Lord's people who are in need" (Romans 12:13). When Paul discusses aid for the saints in Jerusalem, he notes that churches in Achaia and Macedonia "have been pleased to make some contribution for the poor *among the saints* at Jerusalem" (Romans 15:26; emphasis added). Paul's ministry is "supplying the needs of *the Lord's people*." (2 Corinthians 9:12, NIV).

At our church, when our pastor, Jimmy, teaches about giving, he sometimes asks those who have a financial need to come forward for prayer. Then he asks those who have extra, and who feel led, to come forward and give them money. It's risky and a little wild, right there in front of everyone in the church. And it's a lot like Acts 2:42-47. The family takes care of the family.

Not long ago, Carolyn and I were sitting together in church, and I knew that the financial "come forward" moment was coming. I prayed, "Father, I want to give to someone, but there are so many needs. How will I know? What do you want me to do?"

He clearly showed me a picture of a man and a yellow shirt. I scanned the congregation to see if there was anyone with a yellow shirt. There was just one guy in our auditorium of hundreds of people.

What were the odds that that *one* guy would go forward and admit that he had a financial need?

Jimmy gave the invitation to come forward, saying, "It might take some humility to admit a need, but anyone who has a financial need, come forward for prayer."

In a flash, the guy in the yellow shirt (let's call him Nick) was in the aisle and down at the front of the church. Eventually, dozens of people joined him, but Nick was first.

When it was time for people to come give to those with needs, I took Carolyn's hand and said, "I know where we're supposed to go." There were so many people that we had to press through the crowd to reach him.

Carolyn and I introduced ourselves and handed him some cash. I felt prompted to ask, "What do you need?"

He explained that he ran a tree-trimming company, and that someone had just stolen his equipment, worth about $2,000. He'd told his four kids, "God will provide, guys. I don't know how, but God will provide."

I asked, "How much more do you need?"

"People have been helping," he said, "but I'm still short about $1400."

I looked at Carolyn, and we agreed with our eyes that this was the Lord's leading.

"OK, we've got you," I said. "Give us your address, and we'll bring a check by this afternoon." What a joy it was to get to be the answer to someone's prayer. This hard-working guy had stepped out in faith, the Lord pointed him out to me, and we got to give. We felt led to also give the family a gift certificate to go out to a restaurant to celebrate.

He emailed us later that week, explaining how excited he and his family were to celebrate God's provision. They appreciated the $1400 but were even more moved by the chance to celebrate. Who doesn't want to be part of a family like that? Carolyn and I had so much joy in that gift!

God calls us to love the whole world. As we do that, we best mirror the early church's example when we begin with those closest to us. We start with our family, then our church, and then the needs of the world.

Circle 3: Love the Rest of the World Well

At the same time that we love those closest to us, we are also called to find and love those at the margins, regardless of their faith. Jesus's parables of the Good Samaritan (Luke 10: 25-37) and the sheep and the goats (Matthew 25:31-46) show us the importance of expanding our giving beyond the family of God. Our generosity spills out of God's family and into the world as a shining light.

Does that mean we should give our finances to non-Christians? The New Testament is full of stories about people working to bring others into God's family. They argued in synagogues, preached in the marketplace, and planted churches. But they seemed to draw the line at reaching non-Christians by meeting their material needs. In 1 Timothy 5, which we'll discuss below in more detail, Paul wants to make sure that the church's charity is focused on a group of women who have proven needs and proven character. Similarly, Paul limits the Ephesian church's charity to the most faithful group of Christians.

It might sound odd to our modern ears. We've come to assume that Christian missions work should meet people's tangible needs, their felt needs, first. Dig a well, and people will come to Jesus. Start a school, and people will come to Jesus. Over the years, Carolyn and I have funded projects just like these, trying to reach people through mercy.

The challenge, though, is how we treat these people once they've come to Christ, once they've joined our family. Do we continue to do acts of mercy with people who have accepted the invitation? We should!

You may know people who acted one way with someone while they were courting or dating, and then once they married, they changed. That's what some of our missions are like: *we'll love you until we have you.*

That's not what we see in the New Testament. The early church's approach was not: show mercy so that recipients of our charity will come to know Jesus. They offered non-Christians love and kindness, but not as part of an evangelism strategy. They weren't merciful *so that people became Christians.* Rather, they were merciful because *they had become Christians.* Mercy flowed from within. Meanwhile, they evangelized, preaching good news to the rich and the poor. And they cared for each other so radically that the world wanted to join.

The point of generous, Bible-based giving is not just changing someone's circumstances. The point is changing their trajectory for eternity. Of course, God can use hospitals, wells, and schools to do that. But the New Testament church shows us how to focus on eternity.

PUTTING THIS INTO PRACTICE

Not every gift needs to be vetted against some set of rigid criteria. But some gifts require thorough vetting, of the kind we see Paul suggesting to Timothy in 1 Timothy 5. New Testament believers appear to have matched their level of vetting in three ways, according to the length and depth of the giving commitment.

1. Brothers and Sisters with Proven Needs and Proven Character Can Receive Ongoing Financial Support.

When someone needs longer-term financial support, like the widows in 1 Timothy 5, it calls for deeper vetting. Giving money straight to someone in need is rare in the New Testament. The early Christians seemed to understand that often, handing out money directly to people in need is unhelpful. Many church's benevolence funds aren't available to just anyone who walks through the door; there's a screening for need and teachability and an effort to address both spiritual *and* physical needs. Financial advisors have a maxim: Money problems are seldom solved with money.

2. Brothers and Sisters with Moderate Needs Can Receive Ad Hoc Tangible Goods.

When we see a "brother or sister poorly clothed and lacking in daily food," Paul says that we are to meet that tangible need without deep vetting, long application forms, or due diligence process. Note that these brothers and sisters aren't "naked" (as in Matthew 25:36); they're just "poorly clothed." They are not immediately hungry or thirsty (as in Matthew 25:35), but they're "lacking in daily food" (James 2:15). In other words, their needs aren't urgent, but as we care for our family, we can go beyond meeting only the direst of needs. (Remember, this is not your *neighbor* or a *stranger*. It's a *brother* or *sister*.)

3. Everyone—Even Enemies!—Can Receive Tangible Goods to Meet Urgent, Immediate Needs.

John the Baptist says that we should give one coat away if we have two and someone else has none (Luke 3:11). James tells us to seek out orphans and widows so we can give (James 1:27).

In other words, if we see someone with an urgent need like hunger or thirst, we should give the food or drink that meets their need. This is not the time to vet their need or worthiness.

When we are intentional, we bring mercy, which opens doors to relationship. Through relationship, we reach people with the Gospel.

PLACING THE GOSPEL AT THE CENTER

Where we see poverty and injustice, our hearts break. We want the oppressed to find liberty and the blind to see. We yearn for God to heal the world. But a slave's foremost problem is not their slavery. A blind person's foremost problem is not their blindness. *Everyone's* foremost problem is that they need the Gospel. In comparison to our eternal predicament, our earthly suffering is light and fleeting.

Jesus comes to "proclaim good news to the poor" (Luke 4:18, NIV). Did you ever wonder why this is His priority, when the poor have so many more practical, immediate needs? Why not start with economic development or clean water or better education or stable food supplies? Because the greatest gift we can give is the Gospel.

As Kevin in Indonesia says, "Preach the Gospel, preach the Gospel! If good work is separated from the life-transforming power, the saving power of the Gospel, it may do good, but not eternal good. There are lots of people building wells and hospitals. We need to do those things, but we can cure ten million people in Indonesia, and not one will escape hell because we do. We need to proclaim Christ."

As we give in ways that the early church did, we find ourselves connected to new community.

A NOTE ON "FAILED" GIFTS

In our fallen world, not every gift you give will bring joy. There are some people and organizations that will try to take advantage of your generosity. A friend in Ethiopia had been giving generously to a prosperity gospel preacher, only to learn that the preacher had taken the money and spent it lavishly on himself. Deeply disappointed, my friend stopped giving to anyone. At a Journey of Generosity event, he realized that his bitterness toward that experience robbed him of the joy of giving. He said, "We have a phrase here in Ethiopia: Fear of bad dreams should not stop you from sleeping."

Learning giving lessons from our earliest brothers and sisters brings joy. But the key to their joy giving wasn't just *what they were giving to*, but *who they were giving with*. In the Father's family, much of the joy giving comes from true partnership with others in His big family.

7: PARTNERS

Generosity Turns Friends into Family

SOPHIE LIVES IN Switzerland and loves to be generous. I asked her about her favorite recent gifts, and here's what she said:

> "There's this guy that I support from YWAM [Youth with a Mission]. He is absolutely outstanding with children's ministry and teen ministry. He was here in Switzerland and is busy with all his work. I took him out to coffee and said, 'What is your life like with your children, your wife, moneywise, and so on?' And he said, 'Well, I still have to keep my job as a teacher in order to have enough to live on.' I asked him how much he would need to be full-time with YWAM. He said a number, and I said, 'I'm ready to give you that, to release you to focus on that.' We need

the right people to do the right work full-time in the Kingdom…. The money I give allows him to reach out to kids and disciple. I'm part of the adventure. It's so exciting when I get his newsletter.

"I did the same thing with another guy who's serving the Swiss Evangelical Alliance. He has a huge heart for the marginalized. When he sees someone who needs parents or a mentor, he and his wife invite them into their home. It's amazing. He was struggling financially, and I said, 'For five years, you can count on this money from me.' I love doing that."

Sophie is giving in radical ways. She's bridging the gap between the giver and the recipient. She's walking in partnership with those to whom she gives. And it looks a lot like the tight connections that givers and recipients had in the early church.

GENEROSITY CAN HEAL WHAT WEALTH HAS BROKEN

Wealth isolates. Great wealth both isolates *and* insulates. Paul says that those who want to get rich end up piercing "themselves with many griefs" (1 Timothy 6:10, NIV). Most global Christian givers we talk to agree. They wonder:

Do people love me or just my money? I used to get letters from friends; now I get solicitations from ministries. If I didn't pay for the family's nice summer vacation, would my kids and grandkids actually want to see me? Do people laugh at my jokes because I'm funny or because I have money?

The Enemy takes advantage of our insecurities. He loves it when we put up walls, or when we start to question everyone's motives, believing the worst rather than the best. Because of his lies, we can become afraid to enter into true community or invite people into our lives. Even as we interact with those whose love is genuine, we think they are really after something else.

In God's beautiful design, generosity can break down these kinds of barriers. Giving away God's money gives us a platform for connection rather than isolation and for engagement rather than disengagement.

CHRISTIAN GIVING LOOKS DIFFERENT

Is there a difference between the way that Christians give and the way the world gives?

I believe there is—or at least, there should be. In the Kingdom, generosity unites givers and recipients in a family of fellowship. Christians don't give as a transaction—"I give you money, and you give me a good feeling and put me on a direct mail list."

When we follow Jesus, our giving is part of how we love our neighbor. The person running the soup kitchen is an eternal soul, and we'll be with that person in God's presence forever. The development director that comes to visit is our brother or sister in Christ.

We treat recipients with honor because we know God has given us a sacred role in the transaction. How do we know this? Because we are all recipients.

Even Jesus was sometimes a recipient. Think of His encounter with the ten lepers (Luke 17:11-19). Only one came back to thank Jesus. That man got to encourage and bless Jesus, and Jesus received this blessing. When the woman broke the jar of perfume to anoint Jesus's feet (Matthew 26:6-13), He received the washing.

When someone gives you a gift, it can be a powerful experience. Wealth isolates, but generosity can pull us back together. Through Christian giving, friends can become family. I saw this firsthand when I led a ministry for children with intellectual disabilities for several years. Some of my closest friends today were donors I met through that ministry. On the flip side, as a giver, I've become dear friends with many whose work I support. I value the relationships I have built with people like Pedro, who leads a church-planting movement. One afternoon, we were sitting together, catching up and having some ice cream. I told him how much we appreciated that he didn't treat us like an ATM machine, reaching out only when he had a need. He said, "Oh no, I appreciate that you don't treat me like a ministry ATM machine, producing spiritual results on demand!" As brothers and sisters in Christ, we had the opportunity to engage one another *as people.*

Christ-centered generous givers almost never go it alone. They look for ways to use generosity as a chance to connect to people.

As givers try to partner with ministries, they ask me: *How do I develop a healthy relationship with the people I give to?*

HOW I SEPARATED GIVERS AND RECIPIENTS AS A MINISTRY LEADER (AN UNBIBLICAL APPROACH)

Several years ago, I served as President and CEO of a beautiful ministry serving children with special needs, called Jill's House.

Of course, fundraising is critical for a charity, but there was a problem: I really hated asking for money. I hated feeling like I was putting myself at someone else's mercy, seeming like I needed something. And I hated the version of myself that I became when I was working too hard to make a good impression on a potential donor—laughing too hard at their jokes, worrying too much about what I wore to meetings with them. There were a handful that I really loved, but usually I just wanted donor meetings to end.

Before I served at Jill's House, I worked in the business world, where I had separate teams that handled different parts of the business. We had a sales team, a product team, and a service team. So it seemed logical to handle my discomfort by hiring a "sales team" to bring in our revenue without me. In charity, though, we don't call it sales; we call it fundraising, development, advancement, resource mobilization, partner cultivation, or some other euphemism.

I hired people who liked doing the things that I didn't. They would get the money; I would spend it. Perfect! Before long, I had one group of people working with the recipients ("doing ministry") and one group of people working with the givers ("raising money").

In financial terms, it worked. We raised a lot of money and served a lot of families. But in God's economy, my separation of givers and recipients didn't work at all. I lost the opportunity to build relationships with givers and to connect them to those we served. I could have increased the givers' joy, but I missed the chance.

As a ministry leader, I wanted to "scale" our ministry. To serve more people, we needed to raise more money. To raise more money, I thought we needed to interact with givers less personally—to put more layers between the giver and the recipient.

Jobs became more specialized, and our relationship with givers became more sterile and transactional. We wrote newsletters and made videos that told great stories, but givers didn't have a chance to know the *whole* story. Thousands of our givers didn't know anyone who *worked* at Jill's House, much less anyone who was being served by Jill's House.

When scale became my goal, our annual reports and updates start to whitewash the truth. We never lied, but we only told the very best. If people knew the struggles we had, I feared they wouldn't give. That's not a relationship; that's sales.

When scale became my goal, I was tempted to subtly mask our Christian identity so that non-Christians would give to our work. But God's presence in our ministry was our power source and our distinctiveness.

In the New Testament, the goal of generosity is not achieving scale; it's partnering together as givers and recipients in redemption. If we break the relationship between the giver and the recipient, it's a sign that our ministry may be at an unbiblical scale.

What does this mean for fundraisers who work in Christian ministries? The role itself is not unbiblical, but in my experience, it can be done unbiblically. When fundraisers feel the need to flatter, impress, and market God's work in order to lure gifts, there is a problem.

There are many godly fundraisers who approach this work as a higher calling. They connect givers and recipients. They build bridges between resources and needs. They introduce givers to pastors and aid workers serving those in need.

By God's grace, Jill's House hired a wonderful successor for the CEO role. He loves our recipients, and he loves our givers, and he is breaking down the walls built by my inadvertently unbiblical approach.

Scripture has a surprising amount to say about the connection between givers and recipients. In the New Testament, the relational chain connecting givers to recipients was critical. I wish I had known that sooner!

I also wish I'd better understood the three themes about generosity found in the New Testament:

> *Generosity makes givers and recipients partners in ministry.*
>
> *Generosity builds community between giver and recipient.*
>
> *Generosity strengthens God's workers by giving beyond the basics.*

GENEROSITY MAKES GIVERS AND RECIPIENTS PARTNERS IN MINISTRY

If you've ever given to a charity, you've received a thank-you letter. Paul sent a thank-you letter to his donors too, but it doesn't look like the ones you and I receive. Here's what he wrote to the church at Philippi in Philippians 4:

> *It was kind of you to share my trouble. And you Philippians yourselves know that in the beginning of the gospel, when I left Macedonia, no church entered into partnership with me in giving and receiving,*

except you only. Even in Thessalonica you sent me help for my needs once and again. Not that I seek the gift, but I seek the fruit that increases to your credit. I have received full payment, and more. I am well supplied, having received...the gifts you sent, a fragrant offering, a sacrifice acceptable and pleasing to God. And my God will supply every need of yours according to his riches in glory in Christ Jesus. (Philippians 4:14-19)

By our modern ministry fundraising standards, Paul messed up this letter. He violated "best practices" in at least three ways:

- *No Social Proof.* Most ministries want you to feel that, as a giver, you're in good company and that the ministry has broad-based support. But Paul says, "You're the only donor, guys."

- *I Don't Want Your Money.* Most ministries ask you to keep giving. Paul says he does not really want a gift. He's well supplied. He's received more than enough. And even if he had not, God would take care of him.

- *Personal Impact.* Most ministries discuss the impact on the mission. "Your contribution helped us reach more children." "Your gift kept the quality of education high here at our fine university."

But Paul does not report results like number of children fed or meals distributed. He talks about what the gift meant to him personally: the Philippians "share my trouble."

There are good reasons that ministries do what they do. But Paul's approach to thanking his donors gives us a clue that maybe giving and receiving in the Kingdom looks different.

Paul shows us that biblical generosity eschews power and pursues partnership. That's because power can create unhealthy giving patterns on both the high and low ends of the scale.

Some givers believe that because they give, they get to control the ministry. These are *high* power givers. A man in my church once made the mistake of telling our pastor that something needed to happen because "Well, I've been investing money here for years!" My pastor—a former Army Special Forces officer—quickly put an end to that notion.

When I led a ministry, I also had the occasional giver try to call the shots, offering direction on everything from the color of the logo to which stories we told at events to who we hired and even who we served. One giver yelled at my team for showing a video at a banquet that was too long for his taste. Another demanded that we hire *two* of their kids. Some givers subjected us to lengthy applications and public presentation ceremonies in exchange for small checks.

By contrast, the overwhelming majority of our most generous givers were eager to serve, help, and encourage. We became true partners.

Samuel from Nigeria often sees people on the receiving end of financial generosity. He says, "What's important for givers is to put money in perspective. We must not give it a place where it does not belong. Those who receive are not materially second class. That's where dependency emerges, when we think the one giving is greater than the one receiving."

As givers, ministry leaders may sometimes serve us, but let's not mistake them for our servants. They are *God's* servants, and He has given them instructions. Our job is to help them fulfill *His* wishes, not ours.

At the other extreme, some givers do not see their own calling as worthy, and they suffer as *low* power givers. They think, "I can't preach, I can't lead worship, so I'll just work in my cubicle and give money to those who can. They know what's best."

This, too, is unhealthy. God has given each of us more than money. Our pastors and our ministry leaders are our brothers and sisters. God does not see their calling as superior to the calling of generous givers. He gave us all different gifts, but equal value.

How can we know whether we're exercising power in improper ways? In *Money Well Spent*, Paul Brest and Hal Harvey list several signs that you, as a giver, may be abusing your power:

- Not responding to the recipient's calls and emails

- Subjecting a recipient to due diligence or reporting processes that are disproportionately demanding relative to the size of your gift

- Taking a lot of an organization's time without knowing whether you'll be able to give

- Abruptly cutting off funding because your interests have changed

Alex in the United Kingdom says, "A deep relational piece is so key. It's different than spreading money to a broad group and not engaging personally. When we see ministry friends sacrificing under persecution, we want to sacrifice with them. What works in business doesn't necessarily work in God's economy. The directive Type-A behaviors need to be checked if we're to be good patrons. It's deeper work with fewer men to achieve greater things. Bigger bets on a smaller number of people. But that also means that the giver needs to be careful not to abuse the power that they have in that relationship."

Let's look at a healthier model for giver-recipient relations in the Bible, where two givers make brief appearances in the New Testament as they partner in the work of the Gospel.

Phoebe appears in Romans 16:1-2 (NIV). Paul refers to her as "the benefactor of many people, including me." She's a giver!

He also considers her a sister and a "deacon of the church in Cenchreae," and he commends her to his Roman friends. This lady could be home in Cenchreae, taking it easy, but instead, this sister, after helping make Paul's ministry possible, hit the road herself. She joined the adventure with money, but she's also joined with herself.

Most scholars agree that Theophilus funded Luke's research and writing of Luke and Acts. Some speculate that he was a wealthy man in Alexandria. Others believe that he was a Roman official who converted to Christianity. Whatever the case, he was affluent enough to fund Luke's work. What a gift Theophilus gave you and me!

With this in mind, it's interesting to note that the Gospel of Luke uses the word "rich" thirteen times, while the other gospels *together* only say "rich" five times (Matthew 3 times, Mark twice, John not at all). Luke is the only writer who gives us the story of the "rich fool" who builds bigger barns (Luke 12:14-21) and the story of the "rich man and Lazarus" (Luke 16:19-31). Only Luke includes Jesus's warning "Woe to you who are rich" (Luke 6:24, NIV).

Why is this relevant? I believe Theophilus, Luke's patron, was especially interested in Jesus's teaching on wealth. I believe he asked Luke to pay particular attention to questions about wealth and poverty. If that's right, then it's Theophilus's partnership and sponsorship that allowed us to have a much deeper teaching on how Jesus saw our interactions with money.

Like Phoebe and Theophilus, we also have the chance to be full partners in the ministries we support. The Kingdom needs gifted men and women appointed by God to serve in various ways. They, in turn, need the financial gifts that God has given us. When givers partner with ministries on equal footing, something miraculous happens: God binds our hearts together and forms true community.

Around the world, these are relationships of partnership, not power, that we see global Christian givers forming with ministries. Abaeze in Nigeria says, "We encourage givers and recipients to be interdependent. There should be mutual trust and understanding. In those friendships, when givers see results and what the Lord is doing, that reinforces their role as givers and encourages them to give more."

Jeff in the Philippines agrees. "Giving is more about relationship than strategy. You need to know people who are doing ministry and give to them."

For many givers, building this kind of connection comes through personal encounters and site visits. As givers build community with the recipients of our generosity, it often makes sense to go to them and see what their world is like, just as you'd go visit a friend who lives far away.

Sophie in Switzerland says, "There's one thing that's the same for all my gifts: I want to know the person. Even if I have to go to that place in the world, I will go and meet that person."

As we've learned about this vision for giving, my own family has moved away from a portfolio approach—giving a little to a lot of different ministries—and toward finding a handful of godly leaders, loving them, supporting them in meaningful ways, and catching their vision.

Robert, who I mentioned earlier, is a brilliant doctor who loves the Gospel and runs ministries in the Himalayan foothills. He's slept at our home, and our kids have gotten to know him. In ways that we never could have anticipated, our relationship with Robert has engaged our family, and Robert has become part of our family.

"Reaching the nations" is not an abstract concept for my kids anymore because we talk about Robert. When Robert named one of his schools after my daughter, her non-Christian preschool heard about it and took up a collection. Robert's family and my family pray for one another. And now when we say "no" to something our kids want, they understand that it's often so that we can give more to support Robert's work in India.

With other partners we support, our family gathers around our breakfast table for Skype calls. The ministry leader's family looks at their computer in Vietnam or Ethiopia or Cambodia or Peru or the Dominican Republic, and we look at ours in Texas. Our families talk about life, about ministry, and we pray together. It's not perfect. My kids are often restless. The technology doesn't always work. But it's also beautiful and life-giving. The world feels smaller, God feels bigger, and our passion to give grows.

Our partners send us their prayer requests; we send them ours. (One of my friends promised to pray for me today as I write this!)

Our partners send pictures of their joys, like the ones in my inbox right now showing powerful prayer meetings and the first day of school for children with disabilities who haven't been able to attend before. They also send pictures of the sorrows; I've seen a church planter attacked by a person wielding a machete and left for dead, and the car wreck in which God protected my friends.

Our partners text us in moments of breakthrough—God raised up new leaders or dozens of new believers received baptism—and they text us in moments of fear, as they head into dangerous areas.

When it's done like this, without too much or too little power, giving builds community, and it forges new friendships between like-minded givers and recipients.

GENEROSITY BUILDS COMMUNITY BETWEEN GIVER AND RECIPIENT

Have you thought about the economics of Jesus's ministry? We know that Judas carried a money bag, and that sometimes the proceeds from that money bag paid for things for the disciples or the poor. When they found themselves on a hillside with 5000 hungry followers, the disciples worried about how much it would cost to feed everyone. It's not that they didn't have *any* money, the text implies, but they didn't have enough to feed everyone (John 6:1-14).

We also see Jesus tell Peter to pay the temple tax using money found in a fish (Matthew 17:24-27).

The Gospel of Luke, always attentive to pecuniary issues, gives us our best window into how the finances worked day to day. Here's Luke 8:1-3:

> *Soon afterward he [Jesus] went on through cities and villages, proclaiming and bringing the good news of the kingdom of God. And the twelve were with him, and also some women who had been healed of evil spirits and infirmities: Mary, called Magdalene, from whom seven demons had gone out, and Joanna, the wife of Chuza, Herod's household manager, and Susanna, and many others, who provided for them out of their means.*

We see Joanna, Susanna, and "many others" providing out of their means. But notice that Luke does not elevate these ladies. He describes a band of people going from place to place. There's Jesus, some disciples, some people who give money, and some recently healed people. There's not a clear line between who Jesus healed and who is giving. It's a joyous menagerie. (Do not put him in charge of listing donors in the program a fundraising event!)

Then again, maybe jumbling them together is the point.

Sometimes we're the giver, and sometimes we're the recipient. Sometimes we help heal, and sometimes we're healed. Sometimes we lead a ministry, and sometimes we're on staff. Sometimes we serve the ministry, and sometimes the ministry serves us. Givers are not more important or less important.

My friend John Rinehart wrote a great book called *Gospel Patrons*. In it, he shares that behind many famous Christian names—William Tyndale, George Whitefield, John Newton—were patrons with obscure names. The patrons, in most cases, did not fund a broad portfolio of ministries and churches. Instead, they focused resources on a handful of leaders and made big investments in their work. And it wasn't just money; they invested time and relationship. They made introductions. They hosted the recipients in their homes. William Tyndale's patron was a merchant who used his shipping fleet to smuggle the first printed Bibles written in English from printing presses on the Continent into England. That's a committed donor!

Many early Christians built community by extending hospitality to visitors or to the entire church. The believers in Acts were "breaking bread in their homes" (Acts 2:46). Church happens in the homes of Priscilla and Aquila (1 Corinthians 16:19), Philemon (Philemon 2), and Nympha (Colossians 4:15). On missionary journeys, Paul stays with various people, like Philip (Acts 21:8) and Mnason (Acts 21:16). Lydia's immediate response after becoming a Christian is to invite Paul to stay at her home (Acts 16:15). Peter stays in Joppa for "many days" with Simon the Tanner (Acts 9:43). He tells Philemon to keep a guest room ready for him (Philemon 22).

How blessed these hospitable Christians must have been! How amazing to have Paul or Peter as a houseguest!

Christians today continue to demonstrate great hospitality. A giver in Seattle told me that she often invites missionaries to stay in her home. Her children have encountered Jesus and grown in their faith by eating breakfast next to visitors from around the world.

Martin in Germany says, "My friends in Portugal and Greece have a better way than we do in Germany. In southern Europe, if you need to raise money, you *only* talk to your friends. You have a coffee and share your vision, and it's obvious—if your best friend is doing something, you want to help because you're part of that person."

Generosity builds community between givers and recipients. And that, of course, shapes the way that givers *treat* recipients.

GENEROSITY STRENGTHENS GOD'S WORKERS BY GIVING BEYOND THE BASICS

Imagine your family sitting down to a holiday dinner. People pass special food around, dishing out some to each person present *except one*. There's a child at the table who is part of the family, but you have all decided that while you enjoy a lavish feast, he should just have a few simple pieces of bread.

Of course it's unthinkable. And yet sometimes we're tempted to treat pastors and those in ministry just this way.

My friend runs a ministry. His child has severe special needs, and their health insurance does not cover his treatment. My friend's board keeps his salary low, saying that the ministry staff should have a "wartime mentality" and sacrifice whatever was necessary to serve the organization. (Then again, in wartime, soldiers get hazard pay. Perhaps his board should reexamine military compensation.) Sadly, this great leader is now torn between his calling to lead a ministry and his calling to provide for his son.

In small, subtle ways, sometimes givers withhold from ministry leaders. They think, "This person chose to be a pastor, so they should be content with a small salary."

But Scripture is clear that we are to treat those who earn their living from the Gospel well. In 3 John, John the Beloved writes to his dear friend Gaius. Gaius has "extra" and is able to host a group of traveling missionaries. Here's what John says to Gaius about how to treat these guys:

> *Beloved, it is a faithful thing you do in all your efforts*
> *for these brothers, strangers as they are, who testified*
> *to your love before the church. You will do well to*

send them on their journey in a manner worthy of God. For they have gone out for the sake of the name, accepting nothing from the Gentiles. Therefore we ought to support people like these, that we may be fellow workers for the truth. (3 John 5-8)

Gaius doesn't know these men before they arrive on his doorstep, but through the Gospel, they are brothers. John indicates to Gaius that the men will not ask for funds from the people to whom they are ministering. Instead, John wants Gaius to take care of them—not just meet their basic needs but treat them in a "manner worthy of God." These are God's workers, after all.

By caring for missionaries like these, Gaius became a fellow worker for the truth. If someone works for the King, we should host them in a way suited to the King.

In the early church, as pastors and missionaries moved from place to place, they worked hard. Paul talks about "working hard in this way" (Acts 20:35). As givers saw missionaries pour themselves out for the Gospel, they responded with hospitality and generosity.

The Philippians sent Paul "full payment, and more," so he was "well supplied" (Philippians 4:18). Paul, in turn, told the Romans to take good care of his friend Phoebe. "Welcome her in the Lord in a way worthy of the saints, and help her in whatever she may need from you…." (Romans 16:2).

But when we talk about how to support ministry leaders, we must also address the other side of the spectrum: how far beyond "the basics" should we give? As generous givers, we need to guard ourselves against being cheap toward God's workers, but we also need to guard ourselves against the opposite problem: ministry leaders who fleece congregations.

Let's start by making it clear that *no one* in the New Testament became wealthy by preaching the Gospel. In the New Testament, as far as we can tell, the lifestyles of missionaries and pastors roughly matched those whom they served. If anything, we see the ministers of the Gospel living *below* the normal standard of living. Jesus, at least during one season, did not have a place to lay His head (Matthew 8:20, Luke 9:58). Paul knew what it was to "be in need" and to "have plenty" (Philippians 4:12, NIV).

The lesson we find in their example is that ministry lifestyles should not be dramatically more or dramatically less than those being served.

Some argue for long sabbaticals and high salaries for ministers. Being a pastor or ministry leader is hard, they say. But so is being an attorney or a doctor or a waitress. We don't need to compound the challenges of ministry by making God's servants poor, but neither should we alienate them from the community or raise questions about their integrity by allowing lifestyles that are significantly higher than the community.

Several churches I know set their pastors' pay to match the median income of the communities they serve, since they believe pastors minister most effectively when they can live among their congregants.

As generous givers, we get to identify great ministries and ministry leaders and to build healthy relationships with them. As givers and recipients treat one another as brothers and sisters, we build community. And in community we care for one another well.

But there's a joy killer we need to address: getting burned.

Whenever I meet someone who says they *used to* be generous, it's because someone took advantage of them. The giver believed the so-called prosperity gospel or trusted someone unscrupulous. We saw earlier that the Owner wants us to take some risks, but we needn't take unwise risks. We can protect ourselves to reduce the likelihood that our generosity is abused.

God's Word and our global brothers and sisters have given us some ways to reduce the chances of having our generosity abused so that we can experience more joy giving.

We look at the joy-protecting processes we use in the next chapter.

8: PROCESS
Counting the Cost

MANISH IN DUBAI ONCE supported a mission agency. "I was supporting my friend's evangelism ministry in North India. He had hundreds of workers [who were going out to witness in the villages], and he was getting baptism [reports] from them." The evangelism ministry wanted to be able to show Manish, and other givers, what great fruit God was bringing in these villages; the baptism records were, they claimed, the evidence of that fruit. "As we dug into it," Manish said, "it turned out that they were all fake records. [The workers] were claiming that thousands of people were being saved. It's human nature that we want to see people raise their hands [in response to a Gospel invitation]. But now, instead, my friend had to tear down his ministry."

Giving away money well is harder than it seems:

- I recently read a story about a ministry that for many years had promised donors that it used

100 percent of their donations in the field. These brothers and sisters ended up in court when donors alleged that of the organization's $119 million budget, less than $15 million was spent on actual relief efforts.

- Doug Balfour of the philanthropic consulting company Geneva Global shares a story about a clothing factory in Mozambique that had to close because Westerners, with the best of intentions, donated so many clothes to the region that there was no longer a demand for the locally-made clothes. Western giving undercut the region's economy.

- One of my good friends was excited that his gifts were rescuing people from slavery in Sudan until he learned that Westerners "buying" people out of slavery created bad incentives. Sudanese criminals, responding to the newly increased demand for slaves, captured more people so that they could sell them to the West.

- A Christian anti-trafficking agency in the Phil-ippines has been accused by its own employees of repeatedly "rescuing" the same girls from the sex trade. In the tragic cases where rescued girls decided that they preferred prostitution to rehabilitation and went back to the streets, the ministry would "rescue" them again against their will in order to pad their numbers to please Western donors.

In this environment, how do we choose ministries that are genuinely making a Kingdom impact? *How do we wisely vet requests and make sure that recipients used the funds well?*

Harry in the United Kingdom says, "There's a huge element of fear—fear of being conned, being defrauded, being ripped off. That is a big stumbling block for people not to give."

Researcher Beth Breeze, in her paper "How donors choose charities," asked givers how they evaluate causes. She heard a multitude of answers, including:

- "I've got a box…. Everything [direct mail] goes… into the box, and I give to two a month."

- "I'm promiscuous [in giving], I suppose! There's nothing very reasonable or logical about the things I support."

- "I tend to respond if it comes on my birthday or on my wife's birthday. I say, 'Well, you're in luck, you're going to get something.'"

Selecting a cause because the mailer arrives on your birthday. We may smile at this fellow's honesty, but are our methods much wiser? The exhaustive study *Seven Faces of Philanthropy* by Russ Alan Prince and Karen Maru File found that "Devout givers" (those whose giving is motivated by their faith) are "least likely to scrutinize a giving decision. Less than half of the Devout say they spend a great deal of time and effort evaluating the nonprofits they donate to."

Is this the way it should be? Should Christ-centered givers be among the least careful? Of course not. Samuel in Nigeria says, "People want to know *how* to give. That's crucial. Once that's ignored, giving becomes emotional, and it's not sustainable."

Thankfully, God tells us a lot about how to give. The early church had these kinds of questions, as well. And, as it so often does, Scripture will surprise us with how relevant its guidance is.

In the New Testament, we find three themes to help us give wisely and experience joy giving:

1. Do your due diligence.
2. Gather godly guides.
3. Transfer through trusted relationships.

Let's explore each of these below.

DOING DUE DILIGENCE

Paul's instructions in 1 Timothy 5 strikes the modern minds of many Christians as peculiar, but they give us some helpful guardrails as we ensure faithful use of God's funds. Let's study them together.

As you read the following verses, ask questions:

- What is Paul trying to do here?

- Why does he give these instructions to Timothy?

- Why did God include this in Scripture?

Honor [pay for] widows who are truly widows. But if a widow has children or grandchildren, let them first learn to show godliness to their own household and to make some return to their parents, for this is pleasing in the sight of God.... But if anyone does not provide for his relatives, and especially for members of his household, he has denied the faith and is worse than an unbeliever.

Let a widow be enrolled [in receiving payment from the church] if she is not less than sixty years of age, having been the wife of one husband, and having a reputation for good works: if she has brought up children, has shown hospitality, has washed the feet of the saints, has cared for the afflicted, and has

*devoted herself to every good work. But refuse to
enroll younger widows.... If any believing woman
has relatives who are widows, let her care for them.
Let the church not be burdened, so that it may care
for those who are truly widows. (1 Timothy 5:3-16)*

When I teach this passage to Christians around the world,
1 Timothy 5 catches givers by surprise. God has been so generous to us, but Paul proposes such strict rules on his church
when it cares for widows. Why?

The Christian church had cared for widows from its earliest
days, but Paul tells them that it's not their job to support all
widows. He says it pleases God when families care for their
own rather than having the church do it, and that too much
support may turn younger widows into "idlers." With limited
resources, Paul says the church shouldn't be "burdened" with
such charity. Instead, the church needs to "care for those who
are really widows."

Sure, God has endless resources to provide for His church,
but individual givers are not limitless. God has allocated each
person with certain resources, and they need wisdom to use
them well to fulfill their high calling. If we will each "give
an account of ourselves to God" (Romans 14:12, NIV), and
are responsible for "every careless word" we speak (Matthew
12:36), we are responsible for every bit of the Father's money
we steward. That's why He urges us to be careful and selective.

Givers around the world are increasingly attuned to the challenge of finding trustworthy recipients. Some Christians turn to the criteria in 1 Timothy 5. Others look at examples of spontaneous giving in James 2:15-16 and 1 John 3:17. What's important for all of us is to do some kind of due diligence as we give, whether that means evaluating financial statements, learning about leadership, or understanding plans. What needs are they meeting? How do they decide which projects to pursue? How are they planning to meet that need? How do they plan to fund their work over the long term? How much do they pay their leaders? How do leaders use their time?

Here are eight tools that the generous people I know use to vet projects, ranging from very informal to very formal.

1. Prayer and Hope.

Minsoo in Korea says that even though he's an experienced accountant, "I cannot determine who has the genuine need. I need to pray. God helps me make the right decision. I try to follow His work and help those with real needs. I say to God, 'Even if I make the wrong decision, whatever money I give is up to you, God, and I believe you own everything.'"

2. Minimized Exposure Through Diversification.

Alex from the United Kingdom notes that givers respond to this challenge by diversifying. "People are uncomfortable placing big bets. When we place a big bet, we should get personally involved to check on it. It's much easier for people to just say 'I'll send you the money, but I don't have time to get involved.'"

3. Personal Trust.

Many big givers want to personally know the people involved in the projects they give to. Hong in Korea says, "I know the leaders, the pastors or whatever. I just ask them to send me a letter. Just one letter a year describing what has happened and sharing how God has worked with the money. That's just a matter of due diligence. I try to find ways to visit them with some presents or have tea with them. Then it's so exciting to find that, like the five loaves and two fish, God has actually multiplied my gift."

Stephen in Singapore says, "We start with the 'who.' We don't look at the ministry as much as the champion or the visionary. If they're a reputable man of character, then in spite of the weaknesses, if he's humble and teachable, it can change. You won't find a perfect ministry, but we're looking for a humble man with vision. A lot of it's based on trust. There's no way you can ensure. At the end of the day, you have to discern and trust."

4. Minimized Exposure Through Milestones.

Rather than giving the whole grant at the beginning, some givers tie their donations to the ministry's progress milestones on a project. Ryan in Singapore says that for some larger projects, "we have milestones in our funding. Rather than giving the whole amount, [the ministry] tells us their milestones, and as they hit their own milestones, we fund it."

5. Due Diligence Through Social Proof.

Carlos in Guatemala says, "I want to know the leadership, but I also want to know 'who are your other partners here?' If you don't have a partnership of givers behind this, I'm not going to do it. I want to know who else is involved and bring in other heavy hitters to validate this."

6. Due Diligence Through Written Questions.

Pavel in central Europe says, "There are questions you should ask. Keep it simple. There are six to nine questions I ask and then an evaluation after one year. Many individual donors don't have the time to build a big system, and many ministries don't have time to fill out long reports."

7. Due Diligence Through Finances.

Amit from India says, "We have a basic guideline. Are they transparent with their accounting? In India, there are many that are not transparent. We stay away from that."

8. Comprehensive Due Diligence.

Ryan from Singapore says, "We're looking at giving to a ministry in Cambodia, but first we're doing deep diligence. That will give the ministry more credibility and will surface operational weaknesses we could address. We've engaged the best auditing firm in the country. This will grow donor confidence, and dollars follow confidence."

There are many approaches, but the one thing that generous givers have in common is their commitment to due diligence. They understand that sharing indiscriminately, outside the Spirit's specific leading, is not biblical and may be wasteful with God's money.

What kinds of questions should you ask to ensure that you're using God's money well? The most important thing, according to 1 Timothy 5:4-13, is to identify true needs.

Scripture talks often about giving to the needy or the weak.

Jesus tells his disciples "give to the needy" (Matthew 6:2) when He instructs them on giving.

He says it to the rich young ruler when He says to sell all he has (Matthew 19:16-22).

The disciples distributed "as any had need" (Acts 4:35).

Paul tells the Ephesian elders that, by working hard, he has "shown you that…we must help the weak" (Acts 20:35).

He tells the Corinthians to meet the needs of the poor Jerusalem saints (2 Corinthians 8:14).

The Ephesians were to work so they "have something to share with anyone in need" (Ephesians 4:28).

Titus's church was to "help cases of urgent need" (Titus 3:14).

John wanted people who have "the world's goods" to open their hearts to a "brother in need" (1 John 3:17).

But what kinds of needs are we to meet?

God gives us great freedom, but He leaves it to us to figure out who is needy. He trusts us. In return, generous givers use the wisdom He's given them to give in ways worthy of His trust and to meet genuine needs.

Scripture calls us to focus on individuals with true needs. In a modern context, that means that we should make sure that any ministry we consider has a genuine need for the funds we can offer. When I ran a ministry, I knew exactly what I would have done with another $1 million, but I had no idea what I would have done with $10 million.

My friend David Denmark is the executive director of The Maclellan Foundation, a leading Christian grant maker. He says, "Resources drive out resourcefulness." Money changes people, and money changes organizations. Proverbs puts it another way: "Whoever gathers money little by little makes it grow" (Proverbs 13:11, NIV).

It's important to remember that there's a fine line between due diligence and destructive diligence. Givers should not burden good people doing God's work. Time spent answering questions or making reports is time not spent doing what their organization is supposed to do.

One way that we can make the best use of everyone's time is to focus our giving on a few ministries. Alan Gotthardt, author of *The Eternity Portfolio*, says, "Most families could reasonably manage somewhere between one and five strategic investments. For most people there is no way to do this with more than two or three major commitments." Monitoring a portfolio of forty organizations is hard to track.

Todd Harper, president of Generous Giving, once told me that many high-net worth givers move away from personal engagement with causes because "their financial capacity has passed their relational capacity." Those God has entrusted with more money than their family can personally manage often expand their capacity by hiring someone they trust, or setting up a foundation, to extend relationships on the givers' behalf. Together, they can evaluate projects, determine genuine need, and consider any unintended consequences of a ministry's work.[4]

The challenges of due diligence should never paralyze us from giving. Like my friend in Ethiopia says, "Fear of bad dreams should not stop you from sleeping." Instead, our concerns can help us rededicate ourselves to vigilance. We can also involve godly guides, which is the second theme we find in the New Testament.

GATHERING GODLY GUIDES

From the beginning, God's church has been at the center of Christian giving. Consider Acts 4:34-37:

---

4   For more information on unintended consequences, check out *When Helping Hurts* by Steve Corbett and Brian Fikkert (Moody Publishers, 2014).

There was not a needy person among them, for as many as were owners of lands or houses sold them and brought the proceeds of what was sold and <u>laid it at the apostles' feet</u>, and it was distributed to each as any had need... Barnabas...sold a field that belonged to him and brought the money and <u>laid it at the apostles' feet</u>. [Emphasis mine.]

Early Christian givers who sold lands or houses did not give the proceeds straight to the needy, even though that would be the most direct route. Instead, they gave through the apostles. They "laid it at the apostles' feet."

Today, Christians still practice this. Generous givers around the world support the needy through established programs or ministries, and they involve godly guides who can hold them accountable as they give money away. These people may come from within the local church body, or they may be other Christians who can help givers think biblically about situations as they arise.

Ivan says, "For Malaysians, the church or pastor plays a very key role in helping people discern what God wants them to do with their wealth."

Park reports that the same is true in Korea. "We give our money in tithing [to the church], so the church decides which missionaries and organizations the church trusts. People trust those pastors who look open-handed."

There are several reasons it's wise to include others in our giving strategies and decisions. One of them is to balance our emotional responses. When we become aware of the needs of people in our church, for example, it's tempting to jump in to meet the needs. When we're led by God to intervene, this is a good idea, as it was when our family helped the man in my church whose tree-trimming equipment was stolen. But often we're faced with personal needs that we're not called to personally address. Those are the times when involving the wisdom of others is helpful.

When I was a child, we attended a modest blue-collar church that my uncle pastored. A family at our church, whom we'll call the Lees, were even poorer than the rest of us. They would arrive at church with grubby clothes, sometimes unwashed and smelly. When I thought of "the poor" as a child, I thought of the Lees.

Years later, I asked my parents what happened to the family. They told me that the Lees had been receiving gifts from our little church's benevolence funds. When church leaders held them accountable for finding work and supporting themselves, they left. For years, they moved from church to church in our community, receiving whatever they could.

What if a family like that had approached Carolyn and me for personal help today, and we had offered it? What a waste of God's resources that would have been! For the Doolittle family to give to the Lees would have been counterproductive.

When we gather godly guides, we hold ourselves accountable to someone who may have better insight into how best to help.

Recently a single mother in our church, Elizabeth, needed furniture. She went to the church with her need, and our pastor, Jordan, posted it to our church email list. Our family prayed and decided to meet Elizabeth's need. Since we didn't know the scope of her situation, we went to Jordan with our offer to help, and he developed a plan that coordinated our offer with the generosity of others at church. And when some of the furniture we gave required assembly—I'm terrible at that!—Jordan was able to connect Elizabeth with someone in the congregation who's handy. God used our church's coordinated efforts to restore this woman and her son physically and spiritually. That's how it's supposed to work!

And then there's this story: When my friend J.Paul was sixteen, he bought his first car, a Plymouth Fury, and painted it metallic green. J.Paul went to church every Sunday morning, Sunday night, and Wednesday evening. One night, the pastor called for personal testimonies. A woman shared that she was out of a job, and she needed a car to do job interviews.

J.Paul says, "The Spirit convicted me. I loved my car. But the Spirit convicted me to give that car." But still, "I didn't know the protocol [for giving]. I didn't go up to her immediately. I went home and prayed. I had to get my courage up, and then I called my pastor. I said, 'Hi, Pastor. God told me I need to give my car to that lady. I'm ready to do it. What do I need to do?'"

J.Paul's pastor told him, "It's incredible to hear that. But actually, someone else has already taken care of the need. But thank you very much." J.Paul got to obey God, *and* he got to keep his shiny green car.

Eventually, God asked J.Paul about that car again. He sold it to fund a mission trip, and through that trip, God catalyzed his heart for missions. He says, "I ended up spending my life in missions and supporting missions, and it all goes back to that car."

Local churches provide places for people to state their needs, for others to meet those needs, and for spiritual accountability to distinguish between needs and wants.

But what about our giving that happens outside our local church?

TRANSFERRING THROUGH TRUSTED FRIENDS

In New Testament giving, the relational chain is never broken. The giver and recipient may not have direct contact, but gifts rarely flow through strangers or non-Christians, coming instead through a trusted series of believers.

To take one example, here's a passage from Acts 11:28-30 (NIV):

> *One of them, named Agabus, stood up and through the Spirit predicted that a severe famine would spread over the entire Roman world.... The disciples, as each one was able, decided to provide help for the brothers and sisters living in Judea. This they did, sending their gift to the elders by Barnabas and Saul.*

This passage captures Christ-centered giving. The group saw a need and gave in response to that need according to their ability. But look *how* they gave: "sending their gift to the elders by Barnabas and Saul." They moved money through a trusted relationship. They involved the local church in Jerusalem.

Likewise, in 1 Corinthians 16, Paul could have said, "Give me the funds. Trust me. I'm an apostle." But he went out of his way to ensure that the Corinthians knew that their gift would be in trusted hands. He wanted givers to be comfortable that he was handling their funds with integrity. "And when I arrive, I will send those whom you accredit by letter to carry your gift to Jerusalem. If it seems advisable that I should go also, they will accompany me" (1 Corinthians 16:3-4).

It seems important to the apostles that funds move through trusted hands. It's so important that Paul was willing to set aside his critical work as a missionary to accompany the gift, if necessary.

The more we look, the more we find that New Testament gifts always traveled through relationships of trust. Sometimes early Christians met needs directly, especially when they gave tangible goods to those in their physical community. When Paul or another missionary needed gifts for their ministry, they reached out personally to people who could offer hospitality or financial gifts. The relational chain was unbroken.

Sometimes the early Christians gave to their local churches. When they gave to leaders they knew, the relational chain was unbroken.

As we've seen, when New Testament believers wanted to provide relief, they gave *through* the church. In addition to Acts 4:34-37, when property was sold and the funds brought to the apostles to distribute, and the example in Acts 11 above, we also see that the Philippians gave to Paul through Epaphroditus, a trusted brother. "Even in Thessalonica you sent me help for my needs once and again...having received from Epaphroditus the gifts you sent" (Philippians 4:16-18,). The Ephesian church could help the widows mentioned in 1 Timothy 5 because local Ephesians gave to their local church.

Why is giving through personal, trusted relationships so important in the New Testament? From a practical perspective, there were fewer mechanisms for money to travel across distance. But there are other reasons the early Christians gave through trusted hands.

God's purpose is not just to get funds into the right bank accounts. He's also interested in forging partnerships and relationships among His children.

Aarav in Dubai says, "Every single giving relationship I have is someone where it's been a very intentional relationship. They're all people of significant caliber. It's always trust, but verify. There's a huge element of trust. It's relational, but we do verify."

Today, some hostile countries make it difficult for Christians to send money to faith-based charities. If they want to give at all, they have to give to—and through—people they trust. It looks a lot like the New Testament, where funds always traveled from giver to recipient through personal relationships of trust.

Jeff from the Philippines says, "Most charitable organizations here are not accredited. Trust is more about relationship. It's a very relational culture. If you know the people and the leaders and what they're doing, then it's OK."

Colin in Switzerland says, "The Swiss need to have trust in the organization. Since that's hard to assess, they rely on relationship. There's a lot of secrecy in the culture, so it's most motivating to them to have personal contact."

THE CHALLENGE OF RELATIONAL GIVING

I've talked to many generous givers who have a hard time with this idea of giving through personal relationships. "But I can't be friends with all these ministries," they say. Earlier, I mentioned Todd Harper's observation that many givers have more financial capacity than relational capacity.

Let me reassure you here. Relational giving doesn't have to mean that a giver must know every end recipient. It might mean simply that the relational chain is unbroken. Building a foundation or hiring godly staff to oversee the logistics can make an important difference.

For example, I have a friend who is the head of one of the most venerated private banks in the United Kingdom. His career is built on trust. So when he gives, he places his funds in the hands of people he trusts. "If you know people and trust them, then you give money, and they can get on with it."

Another friend took charge of her family's foundation. She prayed and fasted about how best to give the money entrusted to her, and she kept landing on the idea of "relationship." So she trimmed the foundation's portfolio of grants and invested more heavily in a few relationships. She fostered deep friendships with ministries. She spent weeks in the homes of leaders and got to know them. She asked them questions about themselves, and they asked her questions. They built trust in one another's maturity and spiritual health. Giver-recipient transaction morphed into an exchange between friends.

Deep questions helped build deep relationships. Giving money became joyful and powerful for her. The relationships she built restored spiritual health to several ministry leaders, and that was better than any grant she could offer.

Alex in the United Kingdom lives this out. "God in His wisdom has taken the most unassuming, most unlikely people and used them hugely for the Kingdom. We need to find 'blokes worth backing,' but it's often not who you'd expect. We need to be careful. That's why we're deeply relational in our giving. Our goal is to work with them over a lifetime."

Like so much in the Christian life, giving is more joyous and fun when it happens together. How can we bring our brothers and sisters along on the journey toward joy giving? That's Chapter 9.

9: PROMOTION

Join the Journey

IN ONE OF MY FAVORITE literary passages, C.S. Lewis says this in *Reflections on the Psalms*:

> "…We delight to praise what we enjoy because the praise not merely expresses but completes the enjoyment…. It is not out of compliment that lovers keep on telling one another how beautiful they are; the delight is incomplete till it is expressed. It is frustrating to have discovered a new author and not to be able to tell anyone how good he is; to come suddenly, at the turn of the road, upon some mountain valley of unexpected grandeur and then to have to keep silent because the people with you care for it no more than for a tin can in the ditch; to hear a good joke and find no one to share it with…"

Praising what we love completes the pleasure of engaging with it. Generous givers around the world have come to love giving, to love generosity, to love sharing with ministries. They've built relationships and visited amazing ministries. Naturally, their hearts want to share this joy and bring others along. When I meet with these givers, there are two questions they often ask me:

Does my giving need to be secret?

How can I find others with whom to give and with whom to spread the message of generosity?

These are great questions. Many givers aren't sure if they should talk about the joy of generosity. Often, it's because they're confused about legalism.

MATTHEW 6, THE LEFT HAND, AND THE RIGHT HAND

The New Testament church broke the rule. Jesus Himself broke the rule.

What rule? The one in Matthew 6, when Jesus says never to tell people about our generosity and never to talk about giving.

He did say that, didn't He?

Let's look at Matthew 6:1-4:

> *Beware of practicing your righteousness before other people in order to be seen by them, for then you will have no reward from your Father who is in heaven.*

Thus, when you give to the needy, sound no trumpet before you, as the hypocrites do in the synagogues and in the streets, that they may be praised by others. Truly, I say to you, they have received their reward. But when you give to the needy, do not let your left hand know what your right hand is doing, so that your giving may be in secret. And your Father who sees in secret will reward you.

Is Jesus outlining a principle of absolute secrecy? I don't think so. We know Him well enough by now to know that He's more interested in our hearts and our motives than with some legalistic rule.

Around the world, though, givers wrestle with how public to make their giving. Many say, "Here's the money, but don't say anything." And in doing so, they miss a chance to inspire and encourage other givers.

Let's look at Matthew 6 again. Jesus speaks to our motives and our hearts: Don't give *so that* others see you. If we're giving because we want other people to know how much God has blessed us or how much we can give, our hearts are driven more by others' positive reactions and esteem, not the good that God will bring to the recipient.

When you are called to give, reflect on the outcome you envision and lay it before God. If you think primarily of the beauty of offering the gift to Jesus, proceed with the gift. If your thoughts turn to what others will think, it's time to stop. If you're imagining your name on that donor wall or in the gala's program as a table sponsor more than you're thinking about how God might use your gift to change someone's eternal life, Jesus wants you to pause.

But at the same time, He wants the light of our good works to shine. Here's what He says in Matthew 5, just before the "left hand, right hand" chapter:

> *Nor do people light a lamp and put it under a basket,*
> *but on a stand, and it gives light to all in the house.*
> *In the same way, let your light shine before others,*
> *so that they may see your good works and give glory*
> *to your Father who is in heaven. (Matthew 5:15-16)*

When God gets glory in our good works, He wants people to see our good works. And that includes financial generosity. When we give for *His* glory, He gets the glory as others see our generosity. But when we give for *our* glory, we steal His glory.

Of course, we may not want to tell the world all of the details of our gifts, but when we give, the Bible does not tell us that we should remain silent about it, either. God likes to use our generosity to inspire and encourage other givers.

Matthew 6 is a spiritual doctrine of the heart, not a legalistic doctrine of secrecy.

When we open our homes for a small group, everyone knows it's our home. When we work in a soup kitchen, people see us doing it. Those acts are public. But if we do it *so that others see us*, it's sin.

We can look at financial generosity the same way. Do we lose our heavenly reward when we report charitable giving on tax forms? If we give money to our church using checks or credit cards, do we lose our reward when the church treasurer processes the payment and sees our names? I don't think so.

Jesus's own financial generosity was public. He and his disciples gave to the poor often enough that when Judas left the Last Supper, people assumed Jesus had asked him to give a gift (John 13:29). The disciples knew that Jesus had Peter give money to the temple (Matthew 17:24-27).

What about when He did good works? In some cases, Jesus healed in secret, but in many other cases, his miracles were public. Jesus's left hand knew what His right hand was doing when He fed the five thousand people on the hillside. He wasn't keeping secrets, but He also wasn't blowing trumpets.

Following in His footsteps, much of the New Testament's examples of giving were public. Paul commended Phoebe in Romans 16:2 because "she has been a patron of many and of myself as well." Luke wrote about the women who provided for Jesus "out of their own means" (Luke 8:3, NIV), so their actions weren't secret. In Acts 4:37, Barnabas "sold a field that belonged to him and brought the money and laid it at the apostles' feet." The widow who gave her last two coins acted in the open in Mark 12:42, yet Jesus did not rebuke her. And the people who sold lands or houses and brought the proceeds to the apostles did not do so in secret (Acts 4:34-35). Yet none of them lost their heavenly reward.

Like so much of the Christian life, generosity is "caught," not just "taught." How will other believers catch generosity unless someone models it for them, as these biblical figures have modeled for us?

IN ORDER TO/TO THE NEEDY

As we study our hearts, two phrases in Matthew 6:1-4 deserve more attention: *in order to* and *to the needy.*

Sometimes generous giving enhances our reputations. Yet Jesus instructs us not to practice our righteousness *in order to* have people see us. He tells us to be cautious.

Recently, my friend Bill asked me to donate to a fine cause. It's not something that I would normally consider, except that Bill was passionate about it and to be honest, I wanted Bill's approval. Bill was my first boss when I graduated from college. In my heart, I still wanted to impress him. I wanted him to see I'd "made it."

Thomas Cranmer, Archbishop of Canterbury in the sixteenth century, said, "What the heart loves, the will chooses and the mind justifies." My heart loved impressing Bill, so my mind tried to justify why I should donate to his cause.

I asked Carolyn what she thought about giving a certain amount of money. She asked, "Are you giving because you think it's good, or because you want Bill to see you giving?" She was right. Praise God for a wise wife.

I was not giving to glorify God. I was giving *in order to be seen by men*. Or specifically, Bill.

Alan Gotthardt writes in the *Eternity Portfolio*, "Are you trying to impress someone by your giving? Are you trying to create business or personal opportunities by giving? There may be times when you decide not to make [a gift] because you realize that the driver was really your personal gratification."

Jesus didn't just say, "Don't be seen giving." He added the words "in order to." Don't give *in order to* be seen by men. It's a question of the heart.

Similarly, the guidelines in Matthew 6:1-4 do not talk about *all* giving or about *all* generosity. Jesus does the extra work to qualify His instruction with the phrase "to the needy."

When you give *to the needy*, sound no trumpet. When Zacchaeus commits to giving "half of my goods" to the poor, Jesus doesn't condemn him for making that announcement. In fact, Jesus said, "Today salvation has come to this house" (Luke 19:8-9). But notice that Zacchaeus gives to the poor but does not say *which* poor. He does not embarrass any particular poor person.

Sociologists say that poverty robs the poor of dignity. Those who receive often feel ashamed that they need help. The shame is compounded when a giver gets glory for seeming like a rescuer. So even if I have the right motives, when I meet the needs of a specific individual, I should do that in secret. Not for my benefit, but for theirs. Protecting their privacy protects their dignity.

GIVE TO GROW GOD'S GLORY

Now that we know that everything doesn't have to be kept secret, let's get back to letting our light shine.

Our giving sets an example for others to follow. Consider Paul's encouragement in 2 Corinthians 8:1-2: "We want you to know, brothers, about the grace of God that has been given among the churches of Macedonia, for in a severe test of affliction, their abundance of joy and their extreme poverty have overflowed in a wealth of generosity on their part."

Paul uses the Macedonians' sacrifice to inspire the Corinthians. Similarly, my friend Mateo is trying to gather generosity stories in Latin America. "We want to change the perception that the people in church don't have resources. The church sometimes believes things that are not true. It's hard to view the resources that you *do* have. You do have resources. Use what you have. God works from little."

Luca from Germany says, "Giving is very much private, and people don't talk about it. Christians especially. They are doing it, but we need to put it on the table and discuss it more."

When we find examples of radical generosity, it lifts our sights and changes our hearts. Most generous givers can point to someone who helped them along the way. Carlos remembers when he sat down with two older givers in Guatemala. "I got to understand their hearts. They were influential. To me, it was eye-opening to see that this is something they take seriously. They said, 'We're going to be responsible to come before the Lord—what do we want to do with all that money?' I realized that God didn't give me money so I could have another boat, another house. He gave to me so that the Kingdom would advance."

My colleague Mike traveled to Pakistan and showed a video we made to a group of church leaders. It's called "Handful of Rice,"[5] and it shows how a group of poor people in India have helped spark a global missions movement. How? By setting aside a handful of rice each time they make a meal. They give the rice to the church, which sells the rice to raise funds for missions. They say, "If we have something to eat, we have something to give to God." When the Pakistani believers saw this story, their response was dramatic. Pakistani pastors said, "We don't just

---

5   Available at https://vimeo.com/generositypath.

want to send missionaries out. How can we help all Pakistani pastors impact their congregations to live a generous lifestyle?" The Indian church inspired the Pakistani church by letting their light shine.

Martin in Germany points to a giver named Norman Rentropp. "Norman was an entrepreneur and successful publisher. He used to give a lot away to the Mayo Clinic. Then he became a Christian through a Billy Graham crusade and started giving to evangelistic things. He was so well known that he could gather Lutherans and Catholics and Campus Crusade and everyone together to think about these things."

Remember that the purpose of our giving is to produce "thanksgiving to God" (2 Corinthians 9:11) and "many thanksgivings to God" (v.12). Those who see this will "glorify God" (v.13) In Philippians, gifts Paul received were a "sacrifice acceptable and pleasing to God" (Philippians 4:18). The gifts led Paul to give God glory. Similarly, Peter wants everyone to use their gift for God so that "in everything God may be glorified" (1 Peter 4:11).

When we give biblically and faithfully, people see that generosity. Our light shines before them, and God gets glory in our giving. Others realize that radical generosity is normal for a Christian, and they experience more joy on earth, as well as more future joy in heaven.

BRING OTHERS ALONG

Finally, generosity gives us the chance to bring others along. Carolyn and I rarely disclose the specific levels of our gifts, though some know the percentage of our giving and others know what our giving goal is. Mostly, though, what we share with our close friends are the stories of our giving, as well as how much fun we're having. This is how we invite friends to join us in particular ministries.

Generosity can spread through your family, then to a circle of friends, then to the church. It touches weary hearts and breathes new life into them. Generosity finds isolated people and connects them to community.

Throughout the New Testament, we see groups giving together. Whether it's the Philippian church supporting Paul or the believers gathering funds for the church in Jerusalem, giving is a team sport.

Generosity inspires others' generosity. That's part of God's design.

After a tsunami hit Haiti, Josh in the United Kingdom called several friends and encouraged each to follow his lead in giving several thousand dollars to a particular project.

Jeong in Korea has seen situations in which one giver hits financial difficulty and asks a friend to take over supporting a missionary. "They encourage each other to give sacrificially," he says. "Korea is collectivistic. Giving is not only a private matter but also a community matter. Koreans have no reservations about giving as a group. They enjoy doing that and encouraging each other in that."

Stephen in Singapore says, "We like to do giving together. Peter and John found so many fish that they said, 'Come and help us.' That increases the joy of giving so we can give together. We love that."

Tom in Australia creates settings for Christians to discuss giving. He says, "Now they're learning from *each other* much more than from outsiders."

Finn in the Netherlands says, "By giving and sharing… with others, people end up inspired, and they share about their experiences. You remember that you're not alone in this."

Carlos in Guatemala reports, "Rich people now discuss giving in private settings. They're not bragging about how much they're giving, but they're saying, 'What do you think about this project or about that leader?' They're starting to encourage each other in giving. People learn from watching others."

Liam in Australia says, "Now I'm trying to think about who from my generation I should invite to come along. When you get to my stage, you start thinking about doing things of eternal value. How can I create a network of like-minded people who, as we get older and richer, can encourage each other to be generous?"

Alex from the United Kingdom concludes, "That's where the gracious joy of generosity is. It's in that relationship and community of giving."

GENEROSITY IS BREAKING OUT!

Christians open their homes to young moms and say, "We have an extra bedroom where you can stay." Others move into the inner city. Some givers join a 50-50 club in which they aim to give away 50 percent of their income every year. Others set a lifestyle cap.

We at Generosity Path host events around the world called "Journeys of Generosity," which include ten to twenty givers for twenty-four hours. We encourage each other, watch videos that share the stories of radical givers, study Scripture, and listen to God. It's a great way to open the conversation with a community.

God does something miraculous as His children gather around His Word to hear His Spirit. We create a safe space for givers to talk about how hard it can be to let go and how joyful it can be when we do. In these sessions, it is rare for a giver to try to draw too much attention to themselves. Instead, we hear people praising God for what He has done and dream about what He could do. Try hosting a Journey of Generosity with us—you won't regret it![6]

---

6   To learn more, visit www.generositypath.org.

Generosity invites others to share the joy. As you walk in generosity, you will want to bring your friends and family along. Your giving will have renewed purpose. You will find yourself giving more than you ever expected…and loving it! You will find amazing godly people serving through great Christ-centered causes. Your church will join you in your journey, encouraging you and spurring you on. It is hard work, and it's sacrificial. But God's promises are true. Jesus knew what he was talking about in Acts 20:35 when He said, "It is more blessed to give than to receive."

May He bless you on your generosity path.

ACKNOWLEDGEMENTS

THANKS TO THE GENEROSITY PATH team, especially Daryl Heald, Lee Behar, J.Paul Fridenmaker, and Danie Vermeulen for spending countless hours sharing stories and offering helpful suggestions on the manuscript. Generosity Path would not exist without the vision and funding of The Maclellan Foundation, led by David Denmark, and several other generous families, nor could it exist without the foundation laid by Todd Harper and the team at Generous Giving.

To the hundreds of givers around the world who have shared your stories, your lives, and your homes, thank you. I hope these pages connect you to one another's wisdom and to our Father. Thanks to the givers who backed every church, ministry, or missionary that's been part of my journey, most importantly my parents, Allen and Val Doolittle, and parents-in-law, Ken and Alice Starr, for the array of ways you've modeled grace and generosity.

Thanks to all who reviewed versions of this work, particularly the exquisite Carolyn Doolittle. From a theological perspective, thanks to Kelly Kapic of Covenant College, Matt Jenson of the Torrey Honors Institute at Biola University, Scott Anderson of Desiring God, Ryan Skoog of Venture, and Jordan Kauflin of Redeemer Church of Arlington.

Editorially, thanks to Beth Jusino, my trusted editor and publishing sherpa, and to Rebecca Johnson for her gracious assistance. Thanks also to Os Guinness for his well-timed words of inspiration and encouragement, and to Catherine Muthey, who has prayed with ferocity over every word.

And admiration and gratitude to you, brothers and sisters, who face hardship and trouble and persecution and famine and nakedness and danger and sword as you spread the Kingdom of our indescribable Father. I pray that through these pages, God sends you reinforcements to serve in fields that are white with harvest.

ABOUT THE AUTHOR

 CAMERON DOOLITTLE is Senior Director of Generosity Path (WWW.GENEROSITY-PATH.ORG), helping followers of Jesus around the world experience the joy of giving. He holds degrees from Stanford University (BA) and the University of California, Berkeley (JD/MBA).

Before joining Generosity Path, Cameron was a speechwriter and legislative director in the United States Congress and a management consultant at Corporate Executive Board, where he led communities of hundreds of finance, legal, and operations executives at the world's leading companies.

Cameron shifted from serving the most powerful to serving the least powerful, serving Jill's House, a ministry to children with severe intellectual disabilities, as its first President and CEO. He now offers strategic guidance to global ministries, foundations, and CEOs. Cameron also leads the Maclellan Giving Partners initiative of The Maclellan Foundation (www. MACGP.ORG).

Cameron, Carolyn, and their four children now live in Waco, Texas, where they love discipling college students at Antioch Community Church.

Generosity Path

JOIN THE GENEROSITY MOVEMENT by hosting
a Journey of Generosity for your friends. To learn more, visit

WWW.GENEROSITYPATH.ORG

68143109R00118

Made in the USA
Middletown, DE
27 March 2018